MAGDALENA KRONDL

FAITH
AND
HOPE

MY ODYSSEY FROM
CZECHOSLOVAKIA TO CANADA

PUBLISHED BY MSK PRESS

Library and Archives Canada Cataloguing in Publication

Krondl, Magdalena, 1924 –
Faith and Hope : my odyssey from
Czechoslovakia to Canada / Magdalena Krondl

ISBN 0-9781954-0-X

Published by MSK Press

Printed in Canada

Contents

Introduction

In the spring of 2000 Daisy Lau, a long-time friend and former student, gave me a book by the journalist Mitch Albom called "Tuesdays with Morrie", a bittersweet account of Albom's weekly conversations with his dying university professor. Inspired by the book, Daisy suggested that I record my own "pearls of wisdom". My friendship with Daisy dates back to her postgraduate years at the Faculty of Food Science at the University of Toronto, where she was among my first M.Sc. candidates and also my first Ph.D. candidate, and teaching and research assistant and co-author of several scientific publications with me. Her enthusiasm that I should record something of my life for posterity and Albom's book provided the original incentive for these memoirs.

However, I did nothing for three years until I saw a notice in the East York Public Library for Gayle Dzis's Memoirs Course at Montgomery's Inn in Islington. Casting off procrastination, I immediately decided to enrol. Over time, thanks to Gayle's

Author as a baby, with father, mother, brother Jiří and dog Zora

guidance and enthusiasm I have recorded much of what remains in my fading memory and remembered quite a few incidents I thought I had forgotten. The task of writing and rewriting the manuscript proved more tedious than anticipated; it was with the encouragement and help of Simone, my friend and daughter-in-law, that I persevered. After so much scientific writing in my academic career it has come as something of a surprise that even getting down one's memories into a coherent draft is still a long way from having a typescript for publication. I would like to thank Dennison Berwick for his help in this transformation. Over time, my intention in writing these memoirs has become not only to record my own personal and family story but to encourage young people that in whatever situations they may find themselves, the challenges of life will bring good and bad outcomes. The good one must strive to enjoy as much as possible; the bad we just have to learn to accept with or without a murmur.

One of the most appropriate texts for life's journey comes from Hebrews 11: 8-16: "By faith Abraham obeyed when he was called . . . and he went out, not knowing where he was going."

Paternal grandmother Sofie Kodousková-Mrázová, 1855-1901
Grandfather Stěpán Mráz, 1861-1930

Maternal grandmother Magdalena Karásková-Padourová,
1866-1929
Grandfather Jindřich Padour, 1863-1930

1

My Grandparents

Nowadays, all schoolchildren, at least in the Western world,
have heard about DNA (deoxyribonucleic acid, a molecule
of heredity containing the genetic instructions, specifying the
biological development of cells). Yet how many of them, I
wonder, stop to ask themselves how their shared DNA links
them to their ancestors? It is easy to trace down the generations
the colour of skin, hair and eyes. But how do we account for the
more subtle personality traits that we inherit? To understand
these requires more than a static portrait. It calls for stories
dug deep from the sands of time. And though history may
sometimes seem no more real than fiction, nevertheless, all
the generations do connect. Every family member is linked to
previous members, going back through time immemorial;
without doubt, I believe, events of the past ripple out to affect
who we are today.

In the interest of simplicity and clarity, I have contented
myself with delving into the past only as it relates to my

grandparents, who were larger than life and at the centre of my life as a child; yet just as I was deeply influenced by them, so their characters were no doubt formed from their ancestors, environment and culture.

If I think of my memory as a picture gallery, I reflect first on the image of my maternal grandmother in a large oval gilt frame, as was the fashion of that period. My grandmother Magdalena, who was also my godmother and after whom I was named, was stately in appearance, with black hair and blue eyes. One incident illustrates her kindness. One day when I was playing with other children and the boys started to become somewhat boisterous, she took my hand, patted my head and said gently, "Come away with me from the ruffians, my little girl."

Apart from managing the family farm while her husband was away, grandmother Magdalena cared for the many farmhands. She fed them, with the help of maids, from large pots in the spacious kitchen. On Saturday evenings, the kitchen became the bathroom for all the female workers to thoroughly wash themselves in a wooden tub.

Grandmother Magdalena was a devout Catholic. Early each morning she attended Mass and she put her Christian values into practice everyday. In the village she was known as "godmother", as she served in this capacity to perhaps half the village children. In times of need she assisted anyone who needed help.

My grandparents' farm had about 150 acres of good arable land and had been in the family's possession for well over a hundred years. Records show the family were prominent land owners in Vraclav at least back to the 17th century. Between the two World Wars, Vraclav, founded in the 13th century, was a prosperous village with a population of about 2000, some eight miles from Choceň, my home town, and about 150 kms from Prague. My grandparents' two-storey house faced the village green. Behind it was a courtyard surrounded by a granary, horse barn with four horses, cow shed, two barns, hog-pen, carriage shed and a smaller house with a brick oven and accessories for bread making. A small garden with two rose trees, Bleeding Hearts, Sweet Williams and other flowers lay just behind the main house. How I loved the expanse of the fields, the garden, the big, intelligent eyes of the horses, the secure feeling of belonging to Mother Earth, the traditional order of things, the purity and depth of my grandmother's faith. And these have stayed with me always.

I remember vividly the Sunday lunches in my grandparents' home with my immediate family. Food was served in a dining room, next to the kitchen, on a simple oak table with oak benches around it. The room was austere. A large cross on the wall was the main decoration. The windows faced the village green. Next to this room was a lounge with paintings, a rug, a coffee table and easy chairs. Meals were not formal. The custom before the meal was to wish everybody "bon appetit" rather then to say Grace. Not much talking went on around the table while we were eating. Children had to sit and eat properly. The servants ate together in the kitchen. Lunch often consisted of roasted goose, cabbage and dumplings. Draft beer was served to the grown-ups. My brother and I carried it in a jug from the tavern across the road. It was a chance to have a secret taste of beer, as it was not offered to the children. Despite the good food, my appetite was poor and I do not remember whether dessert was served after the meal. When I was young I did not fancy anything sweet. Coffee was served after the meal while the grown-ups socialized and the children took off to play outside.

Sometimes we would stay for supper, and then we were driven after dark in a carriage with a pair of horses to the railway station. Two lanterns, with a candle in each, hung on the sides of the carriage and the atmosphere of the ride was full of mystery, which as a very young child appealed to me enormously. Grandmother Magdalena visited our parents' home very rarely. This was not only because of her responsibilities at the farm but also because she was adamant not to interfere in the young family.

Tragically, she died of pneumonia in 1929 at the age of 63, when I was five years old. She'd never been sick before; then within a few days she was suddenly gone. This was my first experience of a death in the family. It was an end to the unforgettable lunches in Vraclav.

The second picture in a large oval frame is of my maternal grandfather, Jindřich Padour, born in 1863. He was a rotund, jolly man, well educated, a good orator and popular for his good humour. He gained an interest in politics from his ancestors, who played a leading role in regional public affairs. Before the First World War he was a member of the Parliament of the Austrian Empire for the Czech agrarian party. The Parliament was located in Vienna, the capital, and he spent most of his time there, coming home for vacations and campaigns. As a well-known Czech politician after the end of the First World War in 1918, he was invited by the Prime Minister Udržal to join the government of newly-independent Czechoslovakia. Udržal was grandfather's good friend, whose farm was not far from Vraclav. However, this time grandmother put her foot down. She was tired of running the farm alone.

Soon after grandmother's death, grandfather Jindřich had a stroke from which he did not recover. After a long stay in hospital he was brought home, childlike and bound to a wheelchair, to be cared for by a permanent nurse. He passed away in 1931, after two sad years, at the age of 67.

The next picture in the gallery is of my great-grandfather, Josef Kudláček, the most prominent ancestor on my father's side. He was born in 1830 in Borohrádek, a small town near the larger town of Choceň with a population of about 5000. Great-grandfather Josef was a competent craftsman and interested in everything new. In the beginning, he made special coffee grinders, steel cash registers and sewing machines. Later, he specialized in meat processing machinery. He kept on expanding his plant and even added a foundry. He was also known as an expert in gardening and it is a sadness to me that I was born too late to know him.

His eldest daughter, my grandmother Sofie, born in 1855, died at the age of 50, when my father was only 12 years old. She had married Štěpán Mráz, the manager of her father's factory, which he eventually took over together with his brother-in-law. Sofie taught village women to use the Singer sewing machines, sold and serviced in her family's factory. She must have been very capable because at that time it was rare for women of her social status to do any work independent of homemaking.

The picture of my paternal grandfather Štěpán is of a somewhat paunchy old gentleman, though in his younger years he was a star high-bar gymnast. Later, he became the chairman of the local chapter of Sokol, a popular gymnastic and a patriotic organization. A grapevine grew on the wall outside his office and when my brother and I visited him in season, he would come outside with a pair of scissors and ceremoniously cut bunches of grapes as a gift for each of us. We considered this a real treat in spite of their being quite sour. (The climate was too cold to ripen grapes). Coming directly from school we had to show grandfather our school reports. He was always pleased, and would take out his wallet and hand each of us a silver five crown coin. According to the family rule, we had to take it home and put it directly into the piggy bank.

When grandfather Štěpán passed away in 1929, at the age of 67, he was the first dead person I'd ever seen and his grand funeral, organized by his athletic organization, was my first experience of such an occasion.

Though I have pictures in my mind of all my grandparents, I am missing a portrait of grandfather Štěpán's second wife, Rosalie, born Řeháková. She was my godmother, along with grandmother Magdalena. Thus I was christened Marie Magdalena Rosalie. My step-grandmother Rosalie was a tall, slim lady, very kind, with a good sense of humour, an excellent cook and a good pianist. For me she was the most important person among my father's relatives. Her faithful maid and companion used to prepare a tasty veal stew whenever I was invited for lunch. Rosalie always found time to read fairy tales to me, which I loved so much. On my birthdays, when I was small, she always baked a cake for me and decorated it with the face of a little girl.

As I reflect on my grandparents I am filled with a deep respect for their accomplishments, their example of hard work, perseverance, kindness, and respect for others within and outside the family. I suspect that from grandfather Jindřich, I learned the love of my country of origin and a deep appreciation that my roots lie there. From my grandmother Magdalena,

I inherited faith in God and an example to follow in times of life's crisis. Thanks to Štěpán's aptitude for athletics, I may now have better health than other women my age. Grandmother Sofie's gift was her inspiration of what a woman's role could be outside the family. Step-grandmother Rosalie laid down in me an everlasting passion for reading and for living in the world of fairy tales.

I am grateful for the genes inherited from my ancestors. Even more, I appreciate my grandparents' influence in such domains as the sense of family security, codes of behaviour, importance of good interpersonal relationships and respect for elders. During my times with them these values were imprinted on me for the rest of my life.

Author, aged three, and her brother Jiří, aged five

2

Early Childhood

My mother is accompanying our great-aunt Husarová on her return from a visit to our home. I run after them. My shoelaces become untied. I bend to tie them up. Upon lifting up my head - horrors! - above me I see the face of a big man who lives in one of the little cottages near my parents' estate. I scream and wake up. This fearful dream is my earliest memory, at about three years of age, yet even today I can recall it with astonishing immediacy. The dream still puzzles me.

At that time, my family lived in a newly-built house at the edge of the town, only a few yards from railroad tracks and adjacent to the office buildings and long lines of workshops of my father's factory. The flat roofs of the factory buildings invited secret explorations. Nothing was more exciting than to climb and spy on the world, hidden from the grown-ups. I shared these clandestine adventures with our caretaker's little boy, Bohouš Uher, but he was younger and did not enjoy these risky adventures that lacked the approval of grown-ups.

The flower beds and bushes in the courtyard around the house held a small child's universe of secret nooks. The entrance to the courtyard was through a wrought iron gate shaded by a tall white birch. Walking along the railway embankment Bohouš and I would watch passing trains and imagine far away places. From the second floor of the house, we could see the woods and the hill perfect for tobogganing in the winter.

Our family's two-storey brick house had ten rooms. Father needed a great deal of space for his eclectic collection of antiques, which he had begun amassing as an adolescent. Three large rooms, painted in dark green, were filled with treasures: glass, shawls and paintings, as well as military curiosities such as guns and exotic swords. There was a complete set of a knight's armour. This was a great attraction for our friends who would gaze at it in rapture.

Two maids always lived in our house. Miss Aloisie Urbanová, father's secretary and accountant, also lived with us. She was second in command and, though quite independent, during mother's infrequent absences, she ran the household. The house was bright and busy. As well as live-in servants, there was the night watchman, Mr. Hoffman, and father's business friends, mother's personal friends, and our relatives – always people coming and going from early morning until late at night.

Mother spent most mornings dressed in working clothes, with a scarf tied under her chin, walking through the factory systematically making sure to talk to every employee who, at different times, numbered from 200 to many hundreds of people. She knew each person individually, was approachable, learned their needs and met them generously.

Mother was born into an agricultural society that during her life became industrial in character. She received a better education compared to the majority of girls of her age at that time. She attended high school in the nearest town, Vysoké Mýto, followed by Pettingeum, a finishing school for young ladies, in Olomouc, where the emphasis was on home economics, languages, music and literature. Finally she spent a year in a cookery school in Prague, a highly cultural city, where she could go to concerts, theatres, and art galleries; experiences not accessible in her home environment. As a young girl she visited Vienna a few times with her father during his political career.

Mother grew up in a family where the frequent absence of her father required her own mother to have profound management skills. These, acquired by osmosis, were very useful in my mother's own married life when similarly she had to manage the factory and the farm when my father was away. She also followed the example of her mother by involving herself in a number of charities.

The story of her marriage with my father reads like one of the old-time romances. They met at mother's first ball when she was 19 years old. From my father's memoirs, I learned that he was impressed by his future fiancée's clear views and solid common sense, as well as by her interest in his ambitious plans for the future. Long dating was not tolerated in those days. After two or three dates, my grandmother declared, "Mr. Mráz, what is your intention? A girl who is known to have had a previous engagement has no other decent chance of marriage," she told him. My mother's brother, uncle Váša, a man with a great sense of humour, recalled that at the age of 12 (seven years younger than my mother), he had had to

accompany the young couple on their dates and report on
their behaviour.

My parents married soon as my father finished preparing a
house for his intended bride. Although he co-inherited a small
but well-functioning machine shop he handed it over to his
younger brother. With the inheritance from his deceased
mother, he purchased land and built a new factory that in time
prospered well. With the help of his father-in-law, father was
able to purchase a farm in Dvořisko, a village about 2 kms from
the new factory. The farm had belonged originally to the Count
Kinsky family. It was government policy when Czechoslovakia
became independent in 1918 that some estates of the nobility
had to be sold.

In her memoirs mother wrote, "After our marriage, my
husband and I walked from Choceň to Vraclav, about 12 kilometres through spacious flat land which we thought to be ideal for
an airfield". It took another 17 years for this dream to become
a reality.

There are two stories about my coming into the world. One
is that when I was born at home at nine on a Sunday morning, a
band belonging to a local homeowners' association was playing
as they passed our house. This was taken as a good omen.
Another version, spread by my big brother when he was mad
with me, and on the account of my black hair, was that I was left
on the doorstep by gypsies.

Highlights of my childhood include exciting visits to our
parents' farm. It consisted of 300 acres of arable land and pastures, 30 dairy cattle, 20 pigs, 7 horses, chickens, turkeys, other
poultry and even a peacock. Mrs Mansfeld, wife of the farm
manager, who had a house on the farm, used to take me into a
newly-built, bright hen house with individual partitions and an

outside yard. We collected eggs from under the clucking hens. We watched the cows being milked by hand and drank the fresh warm milk. The farm was especially useful during the Second World War when it supplied food not only for my family but also for many other people in need.

Perhaps this is how the connection between Mother Earth and the table became imprinted on me at an early age. In all my years as a scientist of nutrition, the miracle of food has never been lost on me.

Walking home from the farm through the woods was always scary, especially as we had to pass three places with stone crosses marking the sites of unfortunate people's deaths. Late one evening, when the woods were dark, someone leapt out from the undergrowth. It was our maid, Rose, who had a passion for practical jokes. I was only four years old at the time and was utterly terrified!

For two summers aunt Anežka and her husband, uncle Josef Syrový, took us for a few days to the mountains on the Czech-German border. The chalet where we stayed was at the top of the mountain. We hiked through the vast forests and in the evenings had meals of fresh trout from the mountain streams. Then we played chess and a board game called "Trouble" with our uncle. We enjoyed these short breaks with our aunt and uncle as they were so different from the busy life at home.

St. Nicholas Day on December 6th was special for children. The happy day was always tinged with drama – a time of reckoning and reward. One adult would dress as a bishop with a mitre, another dress as the Devil. In those days, railroad workers wore long winter overcoats lined with black fur. The "Devil" would put on his coat inside out, wear a mask with horns covering his face and carry a heavy, noisy chain. The third person was a young woman dressed in white with a veil over her face. She was an angel carrying a basket with presents for all the good boys and girls to receive after prayers were said.

Christmas Eve was the highlight of the year. As the event approached, the house would fill with all manner of presents intended for the staff and for the children of the farm employees. Early on Christmas Eve, my brother Jiří and I would excitedly wait in the kitchen for the signal to go to the dining room, which had been closed off all day. Mr. Mansfeld, our farm manager and as yet still single, waited with us. He was a wonderful teller of tales. Pointing through the window to the birch tree outlined in the dusk outside, he convinced us that the angel who'd brought our Christmas tree was resting in its branches. Then, at the magical tinkle of the bell, we would enter the dining room and behold the splendour of the lighted Christmas tree. The tree was lighted with real candles. Once I climbed up to light a candle when the lower candles were already burning. My apron caught fire. Fortunately mother was near and quickly wrapped a carpet around me to extinguish the flames. Thanks to her quick reaction the episode ended well. Today I appreciate the safety of electrical Christmas lights.

Before opening the presents under the tree, we had to kneel and thank the Lord for our blessings. Then the servants were also called in to receive their gifts. Gift opening was followed by Christmas Eve dinner. My extended family would gather round the table to share the traditional fish soup, deep fried portions of carp and potato salad, followed by apple strudel and special almond cookies. Relatives present included great-aunt Božena Husarová, the sister of my grandmother Sofie, (her other, living sister, Anna Kolářová spent Christmas with her own large family), aunt Anežka, my father's sister, with her husband Josef Syrový, uncle Pepa Mráz, my father's brother, and uncle Václav Padour, my mother's brother and her only sibling. After the supper we cut apples in half to see if there was a star in the middle for good luck.

My early childhood seems like a happy dream, free of social barriers, and infused with a warm glow of friendship within and outside the family. How could we suspect the dark clouds just beyond the horizon? I often wonder whether my earliest memory of the horror dream was a foretelling of the suffering which my family was to endure after the Communist takeover. One thing is certain. The love and safety of my childhood conferred on me priceless gifts. These gave me a life-long feeling of inner security as well as a deep faith in the power of goodness and love, which has sustained me throughout my life, even in times of loneliness and anxiety.

Author's I.D. photograph from Czech national gym association, 1937

3

School at Last

From the time my brother Jiří went to school, life at home became boring and it was a relief when at last I was old enough to join him on the daily trips to school, two kilometres from our house. There was only one elementary school in our town, with separate sections for boys and girls. My teacher was Jarmila Jarniková, who moved with the same class for the whole five years of my time in the elementary school. I was fortunate to enter the first year of her new rotation. Miss Jarniková, even in our days had nice, conservative convictions that a woman's place was at home. Women were to be gentle, obedient and polite. They required the skills of knitting, crocheting, needle pointing and lace making; academic pursuits should be a secondary priority for women, she believed. Thus I learned to read and write somewhat late, at the age of eight. I do not remember how much mathematics we learned.

My life-long friend was Milena Faltysová, a pet of our elementary school teacher. One lunch break when I was seven

years old, Milena and I decided to get flowers for our teacher, so
we picked them without permission from neighbours' gardens.
The task took us almost to the end of school time and we were
surprised when our teacher did not display pleasure on receiving our gift of an untidy bouquet. Our childhood friendship
continued indirectly with Milena's son, Luboš, whose immigration to Canada I had the privilege to sponsor. He, his wife Jana
and his four children, Julinka, Elinka, Barunka and Tom came
to live near me in Toronto and they became a part of my
extended family.

Because our school was too far to go home during the two
hour lunch break, my brother Jiří and I took turns having lunch
either at uncle Pepa's, at aunt Anežka's and for a short period
at our step-grandmother Rosalie's home. All of them lived near
the school. We loved it, as they took pains to feed us our
favourite dishes.

Scripture was taught only to the members of the Christian
Churches. Lessons to us, the Catholics, were given by a very
kind priest, Father Moučka, who could not deal with two overly
vivacious kids, my friend Anuška Hyláková (later with the
married name Syrová) and myself. Most of the time he sent
us out of the classroom. Some years later Father Moučka was
again in charge of religious classes, at the secondary school
in the neighbouring town of Vysoké Mýto. I was a difficult,
non-attentive adolescent, always interrupting his class. On one
occasion I had to produce my birth certificate and when I
looked at the document found his signature there. I ran to him
all excited. "Father, look! You baptized me." He turned round
and looked at me. "If I had known then whom I was baptizing
I would have thought twice," he commented through his teeth.
The irony is that my friend Anuška is now a cornerstone of

the church in my home town. I stay with her whenever I visit. It is the spiritual tie that has held us together all these years.

In those days in Czechoslovakia, German was taught as the second language beginning in the fourth grade. So when vacation time came my father sent Jiří and me to stay with German-speaking families. One summer I was sent to a convent. Another year we went to a German immersion camp in Vienna. At home I also had private lessons in French from mother's friend who visited our family with the purpose of keeping up mother's French. Mother spoke German and French well. Her English was passable.

I also took private piano lessons at a local music school, which held yearly concerts. Mother emphasized that looks and learning were less important than being good. I considered myself to be plain; being taller than all my friends did not help. Thus I was flattered when a boy four years older, Jiří Weyskrab, who played the fiddle, paid special attention to me at one of the concerts. Although we never spoke to each other after that, even now I remember how important it was to me that I could be a pleasing sight to an older boy.

Life was like a fairy tale walking back from school with my true friend Jaryna Jeništová. Her father was the foreman in my father's factory. The family was very socialistic and atheistic, but personally friendly with us. We girls did not care about the grown-ups' political and religious inclinations, thus Jaryna accompanied me for the whole month of May to the evening Marian celebrations at the church. For years we shared the content of books we read while walking each other to and from our respective homes, much to the amusement of the grown-ups. Decades later, when the Communists marred the lives of our family, Jaryna showed herself to be a true best-friend.

The seasons were important to us as children. In the winter the whole family and our friends used to go on one-day skiing trips to the nearby Orlické Hory mountains, over 1000 metres high. Early on Sunday morning, we would set out by train to the station nearest our final destination. In those days, there were no ski-lifts and we had to climb up the mountain to a chalet at the top, where we had a meal and fun. Coming down was again by way of forest paths. I did not know how to ski downhill so I just stood up at the top, then shot down the hill and stopped at the bottom by falling down. I loved it.

In summer there was a place at the top of a river dam where we met friends. There was no fear of infection as we swam with a coin in our mouths across the deep water to a dairy shop on the opposite bank to buy milk and croissants. What a treat that was! We small girls feared the older boys who bullied us by jumping into the river and pushing our heads under water. It was the most unpleasant form of being noticed by boys!

Towards the end of my elementary school years I wished passionately to learn to ride a horse. It meant having expensive high boots and breeches and being driven to the neighbouring town of Vysoké Mýto where the cavalry offered riding lessons. The drill was severe and required riding without a saddle and learning audacious jumps. That year, under the Christmas tree, I saw a big box with my name on it. All excited I saw myself equipped and sitting on a horse. No! The content of the box soon cooled my excitement. Instead of polished riding boots there was beautiful batiste bed linen with fancy monograms; my parents' first contribution to my dowry. How difficult it was to express gratitude to mother who saw me at the age of 11 as a good, desirable bride – completely opposite to my own ambitions. My horse dream did eventually come true with the help of father. I loved horse riding, until the day a horse galloped away with me and I became completely scared.

I write now about those long past years with a smile. Mine was a wonderful childhood; secure at home, with the love and protection of my family (though I was not attuned to my parents' image of my future career), with the joys of life-long friendships and the routines and rituals of school and church. It was a world not yet clouded by fear of the approaching war.

Sister Jarunka, aged one and half

4

Growing Up

Why didn't my mother tell me? Why didn't the teacher explain to me the incredible miracle of which all creatures on this earth are capable – the creation of new life? Instead, this sacred act was left to be profaned by whispers among ignorant teenagers. Fortunately, these Victorian times of misguided prudence are over.

In March 1935, at the age of eleven, I became sister to a blue-eyed, fair-haired little angel. Jarunka was such a contrast to my dark eyes and hair. Once I got over my shock I was hilarious with joy. With great feelings of ownership and importance, I allowed my best friends to push the shiny white perambulator overflowing with silk, hand-embroidered cushions in which the smiling little face was nestled.

The momentous and joyous event of the birth of my sister marked the beginning of vast changes ahead. In contrast with the cosy haven of the girls' primary school in Choceň, I now commuted by train, bicycle or car to a co-educational secondary school in Vysoké Mýto. The train ride was the fun part, and made my brother Jiří and myself the envy of fellow students living in Vysoké Mýto, since occasionally the train arrived late, exempting us from tests. Sometimes mother would send me to school by car. In 1937-39 there was very little traffic and the roads were safe, so I managed to persuade our driver, Mr. Uher, to give me driving lessons and I learned to drive before the age of 14.

There were other changes. The family moved from the house next to the factory to a villa, built by my father, in Dvořisko near the farm. The villa was separated from the farm by a brick wall and surrounded by a lovely park. Meadows and woods lay beyond this. On the horizon, seen from the balcony, stood a picturesque village church and in another direction the tall towers of Vysoké Mýto's cathedral.

By then, my father's enterprise had expanded, from manufacturing compressors and refrigerators, to building sports airplanes. Our farm's spacious pastures were used as an air field. Test flights of the sports planes were carried out by a friendly pilot, Josef Koukal, who taught us to fly. What adventures! Landing was most challenging. Father's willingness to allow us children to pilot his planes was a testimony to the trust he had in the products of his plant. Had we not been too young to be legally eligible for a flying licence, he would surely have used us as part of his marketing strategy.

Meanwhile, in 1937, there were rumblings of trouble in Europe. Nevertheless, my brother and I were sent to Vienna to learn German. It was quite an experience and not a very productive one, as most of the youths were Czech and Hungarian and consequently we learned more inappropriate words in Hungarian than we did good German. Events in Europe were unfolding quickly, and we soon found that our Austrian teachers were far more interested in politics than in teaching us, for, by then, Austria was about to be annexed by Germany. In Vienna, we met our distant aunt Berta Hosselmayer for the first time. She was a relative from my grandfather Mráz's side of the family and kindly showed us round the city. World War I left Austrians in dire economic straits. Teachers like aunt Berta could barely subsist on their incomes. She was grateful for food parcels sent to her by my mother. One day, we had a surprise. Our father suddenly appeared having arrived in his sports plane with his pilot Josef Koukal and took us all on a wonderful trip to the beautiful Austrian Alps.

In the summer of 1938, my brother and I were sent with a group of Prague students of various ages to Kupari, a Mediterranean seaside resort in Yugoslavia. We enjoyed long swims in the sea, table tennis and volleyball, and, in the evening, dances, which made us all feel very grown-up. Once again, father popped out of the blue unexpectedly with Mr Koukal, his pilot, on a business trip to visit one of his industrial projects, this one located in Belgrade. He took us in a boat to visit his old friend, a consul, who lived in Caftat, a town across the Bay. Though we did not know it at the time, this was to be the last "fun" holiday of our youth.

These were the years of Hitler's rise to power. It became clear that our country was in grave danger. So Czechoslovakia prepared itself accordingly. The long border with Germany was fortified with impenetrable bunkers. Our army and air force were equipped and trained. France was our ally. Then, in 1937, Hitler occupied Austria. In September 1938, came the Munich Agreement, whereby the United Kingdom, France and Italy caved in to Hitler's demand for Sudetenland, the name he had coined for the German-speaking districts of Bohemia and Moravia. When Hungary and Poland sided with Germany, our country was suddenly completely surrounded by the enemy and the enemy's friends. Abandoned by France, our principal ally, and with no oil or access to the sea, our country had no choice but to accept the dictate.

In October 1938, Hitler's armies occupied the border regions inhabited largely, but not completely, by ethnic Germans. One and a half million ethnic Czechs were driven from their homes. Our army withdrew to the remaining territory. Our fortifications were lost. We became defenceless. On March 14, 1939, Hitler occupied the rest of Bohemia and Moravia. Slovakia was declared an independent state. That day, my brother was driving with our mother and I to visit her friends. All of a sudden in the distance we saw convoys of grey military vehicles driving against us on the right-hand side of the road. In Czechoslovakia we drove on the left-hand side of the road. Quickly Jiří drove the car into a shallow ditch out of sight. As the soldiers thundered endlessly past, our mother, my brother and I waited inside the car and cried.

When it became obvious, despite the hopes of Messrs. Chamberlain and Daladier, that Hitler was unstoppable and war unavoidable, my father made a tough and noble decision. The last thing he wanted was to have his children educated by the occupiers and possibly face service with the German army. So he decided to send us to England. I remember my father, after his day at work, sitting on a bench with a cigar, thoughtfully watching the sunset, and waiting for a call from his friend Mr. Daněk in England about visas for my brother and myself.

As for us youngsters, we were naive. It is true that for many people, trying to get on with their lives, the significance of the events did not completely penetrate. For me, school and friends were definitely at the top of my mind. Little did I comprehend the gravity of the situation – the German occupation, the threat of war, the fate of my country, the fate of us all. My greatest sadness was that because of going to England, I was not registered to continue in the senior high school with the rest of my school mates. In the summer of 1939, I was especially looking forward to the visit of my friend Milada Bláhová from Bratislava, Slovakia, the daughter of mother's friend from her time at Pettingeum, the finishing school for girls they had attended together in 1917.

In preparation for our evacuation, the summer vacation in 1939 was spent taking a cram course in English. Mother and little sister Jarunka, who was four, went to the seaside in Yugoslavia. Little did our mother realize that we would be gone by the time she returned. Father probably arranged our affairs like this, knowing how much it would break her heart to see us leave with no idea when we would return. And so it was a family friend, Miss Urbanová, and a relative, Mrs Kudláčková, an experienced seamstress, who were tasked with putting together our clothing for the planned "short" trip – a trip that was to last six long years.

Still, I had no inkling of how serious the situation was. In many ways, the prospect of going to England seemed like an adventure. At that time of my adolescence, aged 15, mother was very strict with me because, according to my brother, I was somewhat wild. So I looked forward to greater freedom, and felt perfectly safe in the company of my capable, big, 17-year-old brother. He had visited England once before and could speak basic English. Our Lord is kind when He does not disclose what is ahead of us.

Before departing to England, August 15, 1939.
Brother Jiří, father and author.

Uncle Joe Daněk, Marjorie Hayman
and brother Jiří in Ascot in 1943

5

England and the
Second World War

On the last day before my brother and I left the safety of home forever, our father took us aside and gave us an account of his assets. "All my enterprising efforts have been to secure your future," he told us. His solemn words impressed me deeply.

I was also astounded at the extent of the riches, for in all my carefree childhood, I had never given them any thought. Thankfully, the concept of "wealth" has never registered very deeply for me. My childhood was rich indeed, but to this day I remain deeply convinced that money had little to do with it. My ignorance in such worldly matters was to my advantage, for when later the Communists stripped us of all our possessions, it was not so much the deprivation of wealth that affected me but the human loyalties and betrayals, and the conviction that no matter what was taken, no-one could deprive us of our parents' love.

While getting into the car with our luggage to go to board the train to Prague, our first destination, father's sports plane circled above our heads and waved us good-bye with its wings. According to my brother, who remembers these times better than I, father had our bags sealed and stamped in Prague Masaryk railroad station by the German customs there to avoid any problems at border crossings. We took an afternoon direct train to Hoek-van-Holland in the Netherlands and were alone in the compartment along with a young tennis player, Zora Nechvilová, going to the Wimbledon Tournament. Decades later, our paths crossed again in Ottawa where she was then living with her husband Lubor Zink, a writer and well-known Czech parliamentary commentator on Canadian political and economic affairs.

Our journey to England was uneventful until we reached the German-Dutch border. A German customs officer entered our compartment and asked us where we were going. My brother misinterpreted his question and gave a wrong answer. The officer asked us to step off the train. How frightened we were! Fortunately, Miss Nechvilová, who understood German well, followed us and kindly sorted things out for us. By the time we arrived in Hoek, it was broad daylight and we boarded the ship. The passage was calm. Mr. Josef Daněk, father's friend and our new guardian, was waiting for us with his wife Irene on the dock in Harwich. They took us to their modern, comfortable home in Farnham Royal. Our new life had begun.

Every morning, Mr. Josef and Mrs. Irene Daněk departed early to Windsor. Their factory, Specto Ltd. was producing parts for the aircraft industry. Since we arrived on August 15, 1939 and it was still the school holidays, we were left to our own devices. We saw no-one except occasionally a young, giggling, cleaning lady who did not speak our language. We had no money and so walked for hours in Burnham Beeches, a sprawling park close-by. I picked up a lot of English by reading ladies' magazines which were lying around in the house. Since it did not occur to our hosts that for youngsters, two meals a day were not enough to satisfy, by the time our hosts returned in the evening we were ravenous, but the dogs were the first to receive food. I felt very lonely. Mrs Daněk, born in Wales, did not understand Czech, and expressed displeasure when her husband talked to us in our native language.

On the first of September, 1939, Germany invaded Poland, and two days later, France and Great Britain declared war on Germany. And so ended all hope of returning home soon. I was so homesick that I would gladly have crawled on my knees to our house in Czechoslovakia. In Prague, on the 17th of November, the Gestapo executed 120 protesting students and closed all universities for the duration of the war. I was heart broken but when I cried Mrs Irene Daněk snapped, "Do stop crying. It irritates me. You should be glad to be here and not in Czechoslovakia."

If Mrs. Daněk appeared to lack sympathy, it may have been because she had serious health problems. When finally she was taken to hospital, I was expected to cook the potatoes for our meals. I did not know how. All the hours in the kitchen at home had been spent joking and chatting with the cook rather than paying attention to her work. I was thankful when a kind neighbour, Mrs. Harvey, helped me out of my difficulty with some simple instructions. This was my first experience with the "culinary arts". As a child, I had been intimately connected to the production of food from the good earth. Now I was intro-duced to another important element in the field of nutrition.

One Saturday, Mr. Daněk announced a surprise visitor. As we knew very few people in England, we were rather sceptical. Imagine our amazement when the doorbell rang, the door opened and there, standing before us like an apparition, was our friend of the skies, Mr. Koukal, in an RAF uniform! Josef had begun as an apprentice in my father's factory, before leaving at the appropriate age to join the air force and became a fighter pilot. When my father founded his airplane factory, Josef was its first test pilot. How we looked forward to the joyrides he took us on in the small two-seater plane, and receiving our first flying lessons. When war broke out, Josef had fled to Poland and when it fell to Russia he escaped and made his way by a tortuous and adventurous route via Rumania and Palestine to England. He flew with the famous RAF 110th Czech fighter squadron in the Battle of Britain. Josef was our first and only contact with our home. We did not want him to leave.

When September came, my brother and I travelled every-day by bus to go to school in Slough. I was enrolled in a private school for girls called Halidon House. We wore uniforms with pale grey tunics, white blouses, ties and green blazers with white stripes. The school badge was a water lily and the school song started with, "Like water lilies we want to beeee". Halidon House was not particularly strong academically, but we were taught Christian values, plenty of Scripture and lots of physical education. It was the only place where I actually won a trophy for a best achievement, in the high jump at an athletic competition; the form of the trophy I received was a pen knife. Although I lost it long ago, the pride of being the best at something was one of life's sweet moments that I have never forgotten.

A great blessing at this time was my good fortune to find in this school, even in my own class, Hanna Brunerová, another Czech girl, who was very bright and kind. Having arrived the year before me she spoke English well and helped me a lot. Hanna, an only child, had been sent by her parents, wealthy Prague Jews, to her uncle in Torquay. She never saw her parents again as they were killed in a concentration camp. Twenty years later, we met again in Canada where again she helped me a great deal. Our friendship lasted till her death in 1988. (From our common friend Deidre Knight I have learned that our old school was demolished in the 1960s when the city of Slough expanded.)

With the war, all materials became scarce. Envelopes were reused. Bus tickets were recycled. My brother Jiří once got off a bus from Farnham Royal and realized that he had not recycled his ticket. Dutifully, he ran after the departing bus. The driver saw him and stopped. Jiří got on the bus, put the ticket into the container and stepped off pleased to have done the right thing; only then did he realize he'd deposited his return ticket.

One of the greatest good fortunes in my life, and 27 years later of the good fortune of my son Jiří, was meeting Mrs Marjorie Hayman, the neighbour of our guardian Mr Josef Daněk. She was a Quaker and a Red Cross nurse by profession. Because Mrs Irene Daněk's health was poor, it was decided that I should go to a boarding school. It was Marjorie who recommended St. Christopher's, a private boarding school in Letchworth, about 30 miles from London. St. Christopher's was a progressive, co-educational school with a good reputation. The headmasters, Mr. and Mrs Lyn Harris, were Quakers and vegetarians. Their values influenced the spirit and the catering of the school. The emphasis was on healthy living. This meant plunging into a cold bath early in the morning and running round the spacious school grounds before a breakfast of muesli mixed with grated carrots and, no doubt, grass clippings.

For the first time, I was challenged concerning matters of faith. A tall, red-haired boy, Muir Wilson, asked me, "Do you really believe in God?" I opened my mouth with surprise, for his question suggested that he was a pagan. How could that be? He was white. As far as I knew, all pagans were black, like the little statue of a black child with a money box at his feet standing at the back of the church at home, raising money for missionaries in Africa. When we put a coin into the box, the child's head tipped forward in thanks. In my naivety I differentiated believers by colour.

With all the men called up for military service there was a great demand for help on farms and as part of the war effort we went fruit picking in Hereford. It was rustic living in tents. Rain fell steadily for the whole two weeks we spent there. One night I woke up in horror with a frog resting on my chest.

Fruit-picking led to another lifetime friendship. Elizabeth McCaig, head girl of our school and tennis captain, honoured me greatly by inviting this newcomer and "friendly alien" to play tennis with her. After several weeks, she invited me to visit her father's farm, Barnultoch, in Stranraer, Scotland. I accepted gladly and continued to visit the family for years afterwards.

In 1941, on my way to Stranraer I boarded the train in King's Cross an hour before the time of departure. The train was empty. I was tired, so I stretched out on the bench and fell asleep. When the movement of the train woke me I was astounded to find the compartment full of soldiers sitting everywhere, even up in the luggage rack, yet leaving me to occupy a whole bench without waking me. What consideration and politeness! I was quite touched, as I would not have expected such behaviour from the soldiers. Yet that was England during the war!

The need for workers was especially great at harvest time. On one occasion my brother and his college friend Olgier Zienkiewicz came to help. Another time Jiří Honig, a Czech friend from my home town, serving in the army, joined us. Occasionally, Elizabeth McCaig's cousins from Edinburgh were there as well. The fun we had more than made up for the hard work. And how well we ate! Mrs McCaig used to cook on an open fire for 20 hungry people. Her food was delicious, especially the home-made scones, pancakes, angel cakes, served with fresh cream, theirs being a dairy farm. During harvest time, the incredible lady started cooking at 3:00 am and went to bed at 1.00 am. When the harvest was in, she collapsed and slept for two days in a row. She was not a typical farmer's wife perhaps; her interest was music, and somehow she found time to play the harp. After her retirement, she went to Italy to learn the language.

On Sunday all the young people used to bicycle to the nearby coast to swim. Once, we narrowly escaped drowning, as the current took us from the sandy beach into the open sea close to needle-sharp rocks. Thanks to the strength of Olgier, who pulled the weaker ones on the rocky shore, a major tragedy was avoided. We all returned to the farm not daring to mention our close escape to the grown-ups in case they forbade us to go again. We were exhausted from the ordeal and next day our work performance did not please Mr. McCaig.

On the farm in the summer of 1942 I pricked my thumb on a thistle. The finger became extremely inflamed. Elizabeth McCaig's sister, Eleanor, who was a registered nurse and on leave from her war duties, treated it, but my thumb refused to heal. When my brother and I were invited to Edinburgh by Elizabeth's cousin, Sandy McWilliam, I was loathe to miss the opportunity and was not going to let a sore thumb stop me. However, when we arrived, the pain was so very bad that the local doctor suggested amputating my hand. Fortunately my brother took charge. He took me back to Marjorie Hayman, our guardian's neighbour in London. She took me to the hospital where Dr. Fleming was conducting clinical trials of a new wonder drug – penicillin. It saved my hand.

My friendship with Elizabeth lasted until her death in the 1990's; my link to the family continues, especially with her daughters Sheena and Lindsey and sisters Margaret and Eleanor. Another friend and poet from St. Christopher's School, Margaret Smith, graduated one year before me. I used to visit her at Cambridge University on my bicycle where she snuck me into her dormitory for the night, against the rules. Alice Little, another friend, whose family welcomed me into their home, wrote a book about her stay in Africa. Both Margaret and Alice have passed on now. Other friendships continue to this day. Anthony Lane who was a special friend, married a Czech girl, Hana. We met again in 1998.

I left St. Christopher's in 1940 with a sad heart and deep gratitude for the friendships I had made there. The sense of belonging, the fun and adventures, the laughter – all of these fortified me and made it easier to bear the difficult times. Grim nights spent in a provisional shelter during air-raids, when the sky over the school fields was red with the blaze of London burning, could not mar the feeling that I was blessed. St. Christopher's gave me what I needed most at the time of life when friendship is of utmost importance.

6

The University Years

The happy years at the very progressive, co-ed St. Christopher's ended with something of an anti-climax. Upon my graduation, my guardian, Mr Daněk, or uncle Joe as we now called him, announced that I would now go to a domestic science college. My heart dropped. Homemaking was the last thing in the world I wanted to study. No doubt this was indeed what my mother would have wanted. Given the opportunity, certainly I would have protested but because of the war, it was not possible to actually discuss this with my parents. Uncle Joe was doing his utmost to direct us as he thought my mother and father would have wanted.

Thank God, Marjorie Hayman once again came to my rescue by suggesting that I attend King's College of Household and Social Science, (KCHSS), London University. I enrolled there in 1941. KCHSS was in accord with the sorts of ideas Marjory Hayman stood for. It was a women-only university and had originated as a result of the feminist movement in the post

45

Students at King's College of Household and Social Science, 1944:
Top row, l-r, Freda Cowell, Ivy Hughes, Dorothy Reed,
Jocelyn Patterson, author; middle row l-r, Julia Tall, Shirley Taylor,
Monica Chettle, Mary Costain, bottom row l-r, Mollie Smart,
Margaret Livesey, Elizabeth Nash, Margaret Harrison

Victorian era. The first B.Sc. degrees were granted to the College by London University in 1920. During the 1938-1939 sessions, on account of the threat of war, the British Government decreed that colleges would have to be evacuated from dangerous locations, especially London. KCHSS first found accommodation at the University College, Cardiff, in Wales, but the danger of air-raids forced another move in 1940 to University College, Leicester. In 1953, by Royal Charter, men were admitted and the name was changed to Queen Elizabeth College. At that time, the Queen Mother, after whom it was named, wrote, "The College has enjoyed a long and happy association with the Royal Family".

As it turned out, the program of the College of Household and Social Science consisted of a blend of economics and basic sciences. Although the concept of household science was not held in high esteem by feminists at that time and was very slowly being dismantled, the fact is that it opened the way to higher learning for women in fields such as nutrition and various social sciences.

For me, the great advantages of the program were the laboratory courses in chemistry, biology, histology and physics. I still remember how I had to overcome my abhorrence of dissecting earthworms. The generosity of Leicester chemistry students included sharing their laboratory space with us. This offered an opportunity for their extra coaching in analytical methods, which sometimes exceeded the recommendations of the chemistry professor Dr. Tinkler.

One of the unforgettable incidents occurred in a physics lecture by Professor Dillan. Our program was strictly female-only, but during the war some courses were attended by young officers. Once, to their bewilderment, Prof. Dillan sneezed while pointing to the blackboard and nonchalantly lifted up her long skirt to fish out a handkerchief from her bloomers. The manners, fashion and social context changed drastically in the following years.

Not all the professors moved with KCHSS to Leicester. Many commuted from London for the day of their lectures along with their travelling cases. A psychology professor, Mr. Timoshenko, a Russian by origin, tried to demonstrate the power of love, by embracing his spacious travelling case and pressing it to his slender bosom. We were too polite to express loudly our amusement.

When I arrived in Leicester, there were no vacancies in the King's College residency. The next best accommodation was a mansion housing the domestic science students. The food was served with a refinement that would have satisfied royalty, but in quantities that would barely sustain a person on a weight reduction program. Young ladies there were expected to learn the graces and accomplishments necessary to attract a husband rather than to develop any intellectual notions. My escape was in reading "Whiteoaks of Jalna" by Mazo de la Roche, a novel describing the life of early settlers, race-horse breeders, in Toronto. I never dreamed that I would one day move to live there.

While looking for somewhere else to live, I was approached by one of the elite students, Dorothy Reed, with an offer to share lodgings. Being the only "allied alien" at the college and rather shy, I was flattered and elated. However, her offer did not come out of the blue. Dorothy had attended a high school in Hitchin, a neighbouring town to Letchworth, where I had gone to St. Christopher's. She had read in the St. Christopher School magazine an article I had written about the German invasion of

Czechoslovakia. When she heard at roll-call on the first day in college the name Mrázová, my maiden name, she remembered the article, and was curious to know me. So began a life-long friendship and an intertwining of many lives over the years, especially with Freda Cowell, Barbara Bradley, Shirley Taylor and Joan Welsh. I've been fortunate to meet Louise Davies, who is also an academician, a few times at international nutrition conferences.

For three years I was blessed to have Dorothy's help with my studies. Although we were of different backgrounds and temperaments, we enjoyed each other very much and so we shared a good many lodgings and even more laughs. At one "digs" our landlords had a very boisterous, noisy little boy called Nigel. Imagine our horror when we returned from Christmas holidays and the little rascal rushed to us to boast about his Christmas present – a megaphone! At another family, there were two little boys. Their father was away in the RAF. Food was rationed. Often when supper was finished the smaller boy would say, "I'm still hungry". Dorothy and I were also still hungry so we started smoking to curb our appetites. When we returned from vacation, I brought along some dry salami sausage, a gift from uncle Joe, and we would chew slices of it. One day, my brother, Jiří, serving with the RAF, dropped in before leaving for France. Our landlady didn't quite know how to handle this visit from a "strange man". By coincidence, the day we were to sit down to write our final examinations was the 6th of June 1944 – D-Day, the first day of the allied invasion of Europe. Needless to say, our exams paled in comparison to the importance of this event.

In truth, it must be said that I did not properly appreciate the value of what I was learning at King's College. As it turned out though, those years provided me with an excellent education in basic sciences and a solid foundation for the field of nutrition, which was to become my life-long profession. At that time, I believed my talents lay more in the social sciences and for this reason I spent one month each summer working at the residence of the Time and Talent Settlement, located in frail buildings shattered by bombing, in a poor area of London Docks near Elephant and Castle. Social work was being done under the auspices of women from aristocratic circles and the Church of England. During the second summer I shared accommodations with a lady who was an air raid warden. As soon as I arrived the air-raid sirens sounded and she disappeared to do her job without even telling me where the shelter was. As everyone else was already hiding, there was nobody to ask. I was in a building right next to an anti-aircraft cannon and the base of searchlights, thus a perfect bombing target. When the bombs started falling, I thought, "For sure this is the end." Then and there, I promised the Lord that if I survived, I would go to church. I survived that night and true to the bargain I had made with the Almighty, I began going to church regularly, though it took years before I truly appreciated the power of prayer. Today, I believe I survived thanks to the prayers of my mother.

During one summer holiday, as part of the war effort, I worked in uncle Joe's factory in Windsor. At that time, I lived in uncle Joe's house in Ascot, situated near the famous horse racing course. The house was rented from the Queen, a restored old country villa with spacious grounds fenced by rhododendrons with nesting nightingales, the awesome night time singers. From Ascot I had to bicycle through Windsor Park to reach the factory. On more than one occasion, the King and

Princesses Elizabeth and Margaret rode by on their horses. Once, they rode near enough to see me and replied gracefully to my greeting.

In those days, I had two boyfriends. The first one was Tony Boaz Jarret, a friend of my brother. For a long time we were pen pals. He was a mechanical engineer who also loved biology and art. I was flattered when he sent me a picture of an Amoeba, the most primitive form of life, taken through a microscope. On the back, he wrote, "The second most fascinating image on earth". He enrolled in the Royal Navy and after the war married a Hungarian girl.

The second boyfriend was Jiří Honig, a former student in my Czech secondary school and three years my senior who'd never taken much notice of me. When a local group of Czechs living in Leicester held a national memorial service, I was asked to recite a poem. Two busloads of soldiers from the Czechoslovak Army Unit stationed nearby attended the service. When it ended, I invited the officers-in-charge to bring the young men to join our College dance held that evening. The dance turned out to be a real success. I also learned that an absent member of their unit was a native from my home town. It was Jiří. Later he came to visit me in Leicester and soon after this meeting, his unit was sent to invade Normandy. We wrote to each other. In France, he was seriously injured and, after the war, married a nurse whom he met while in hospital. Since that time we have remained friends.

University life during the war was certainly different and in many ways, possibly more eventful than it would have been in peacetime. The Second World War continued for another year after my graduation. And so it was still another year before my brother Jiří and I could return home.

Brother Jiří and uncle Joe Daněk in RAF uniforms
at the end of Second World War

7

The Last Year of the War

My university years ended when I graduated with a B.Sc. in 1944; then I had to face the real world. During the war there was a shortage of professionals in every field of specialization, thus I received a number of job offers. But Mr. Frank Knecht, a friend of my guardian Mr. Daněk, convinced me that it was my patriotic duty to work for the Czechoslovak government-in-exile. The government was located in the centre of London, in a high-rise building called Furstcroft. I had met the President, Dr. Eduard Beneš, in the fall of 1939, at the beginning of the war when my brother and I accompanied our guardian, a well-known figure among Czech exiles, to a dinner party. On that occasion I was seated next to the wife of the President, Hana Beneš. She was very gentle, a real lady and she showed sincere sympathy to a girl who at that time was desperately homesick. Other guests at the dinner included the Czech foreign minister, Jan Masaryk, son of Czechoslovakia's first president, Tomáš Garigue Masaryk. Jan was a very influential diplomat who's life ended tragically after he returned to Prague.

For a while I worked in the Ministry of Foreign Affairs of the Czechoslovak government-in-exile as a translator of Czech broadcasts into English for the benefit of the English censors. Once I was called in to the head of the department, Joseph Korbel who reprimanded me for wrongly translating a word as "flange" instead of "wing". Apparently, this could have had serious international consequences. Half a century later I learned that Joseph Korbel was the father of Madeleine Albright, the US Secretary of State under President Bill Clinton. Other well-known Czech politicians in the broadcasting section at that time included Dr. Klementis, who was executed on his return to Prague in 1948. He belonged to the Communist faction advocating participation in the Marshall Plan, the economic reconstruction plan funded by the United States after the Second World War. When other Communists loyal to the hegemony of the Soviet Union took control they liquidated the opposing faction of which he was a member.

As a translator I could not utilize my knowledge of nutrition acquired at university, so I was fortunate to be transferred from the Ministry of Foreign Affairs to the Ministry of Reconstruction. This placement offered me the opportunity of contact with the British Ministry of Food. There I gained experience in methodology of food consumption surveys and in the development of recommended daily intakes of nutrients as the basis for determining food rations for the general public, as well as for the military personnel and for communal feeding. With a government food inspector as my tutor, I visited coal mines in Ayrshire, Scotland. One unique experience was at a military weapons factory located underground. No metal objects were allowed and I had to take out all my hairpins. My internship with the Ministry of Food gave me the opportunity to learn about the differences in the feeding systems used by the American and British armies. The former had packaged fortified food parcels, the latter field kitchens. The experience gained at the British Ministry of Food was most useful after my return to Prague.

Meanwhile Jiří, my brother, was in the Air Force and depressed by the long wait for an appointment. I was worried about him, as he was not just my only family in England but also the closest person on whom I could always rely. He shared his allowance with me during my years of study, as uncle Joe was more generous to him, a man, than to me, a girl. I visited him once or twice at his base. It was marvellous when he was on leave on New Year's Eve 1944 and we both stayed at Marjorie's house in London. In the evening we went to celebrate with Jiří's Polish friend Olgier at a restaurant full of Polish officers in the centre of the city. The evening was great until it came time to pay. As, at that time, I was earning a good salary it was on me to pay for the supper. Scatter-brained, I'd forgotten my purse and Jiří had to pawn his watch to save the situation. We left the restaurant with just enough time to catch the last Underground train at midnight. The train was in when we rushed onto the platform and Jiří immediately jumped in. Suddenly, the doors closed and the train departed. I had to walk home alone to Ealing, many miles from the centre of the city. However, I was not frightened as there was not much crime during the war.

Early in 1945 Jiří was transferred to London to attend a course in meteorology. We shared the sublet of an apartment of a Czech officer and his wife, a medical doctor. The end of the war was in the air. Sometimes we walked on the Hampstead Heath and discussed the future. We feared that our parents might have been persecuted by the Germans for having

children in England and that they might not be alive. We hoped
our little sister Jarunka would have survived. I was to go home
first, find her, and bring her to England and from there
the three of us would emigrate to Canada. Jiří could not leave
England while he was waiting to be released from service with
the Royal Air Force.

VE Day arrived – the end of the war in Europe. People were
ecstatic. Uncle Joe phoned us to celebrate with him at a restaurant on the river Thames at Marlow. That night is unforgettable. No-one was a stranger; everyone became a friend –
singing, dancing, and embracing each other, happy and exalted
with joy.

Immediately afterwards I joined the first airlifted medical
expedition returning to Czechoslovakia. Each of us received
clothes coupons, as a courtesy of British government. I meant
to use them for gifts of textiles for the family but I lost them.
What bad luck. The hundred of us in the medical expedition
cleared Customs in the airport. Of course everyone was very
excited about returning to our home country, only to be turned
away because there was no clearance for our plane to take off.
This was repeated for five days in a row.

Finally we left London for Prague on June 2, 1945. Our pilot
was Captain Nedvěd, whom I'd met before, as he was the
husband of one of my London gym friends. The flight was quite
an adventure with all the foreseen difficulties of postwar confusion. We were seated in the 100-seat Boeing plane arranged
for military purposes with seats along the sides of the plane
instead of the usual style for civilian passengers. The plane had
to stop in Brussels, where our medical team was expected to
pass delousing procedures, demanded for all repatriates, as
most were arriving from concentration camps. Finally our air

transport ended in Plzeň, Czechoslovakia, where the US army was in charge. Prague was under the protection of the Soviet Army. The significance of the adventure, great at that time, quickly faded in light of the things to come.

Returned home in 1945, at the villa in Dvořisko with father,
mother, sister Jarunka and our dog Rek

8

Returning Home

Returning home to a Czechoslovakia liberated from German occupation, it was dissapointing to be welcomed by American soldiers instead of by our own countrymen. In England during the war American soldiers were not popular on account of showing off with their food and money, and because of their rowdy behaviour.

Our expedition was transported from the airfield to the city and there in the city hall of Plzeň we found ourselves in the middle of a formal ball to celebrate the end of the war. Wearing our crumpled travelling clothes, we watched the smart crowd dancing in their best evening attire. I was surprised by an invitation to dance from a good-looking man called Maximilian who'd recently returned from a concentration camp. His name seemed peculiar to me as it reminded me of the name of a bull on our farm. But that evening, the dance belonged to the festive mood of coming home.

After some delay waiting for a train passage, we at last arrived in Prague, a strange city for a seasoned Londoner.

Members of our expedition, all ideological Communists, went directly to the Communist headquarters at Prašná Brána to report to the MP Anežka Hodinová-Spurná. The latter arranged for the women of the expedition temporary accommodation in the Women's Hostel.

The main post office was near these headquarters and I went there to try to phone our home in Choceň. My call was received by Miss Aloisie Urbanová, my father's administrator. Miss Urbanová was like an aunt to me, as she'd lived in my parents' house since my birth. I was surprised when she asked me about my husband. I had not yet even entertained the idea of getting married. I found out later that her question was triggered by fabricated information about my brother's and my life sent in mysterious letters that our parents had been receiving during the war by way of an alleged underground organization. These had been written and delivered by a kind person, Mr. Škorpil, probably wanting to relieve our parents' pain of having no news of us for so many years.

Miss Urbanová directed me to Bohumil Hubschman, an architect, whose wife was a younger sister of my mother's brother's wife, Jarmila. There I was to receive the first briefing of the current situation; father had been taken into custody by the Communist revolutionary council's chairman in Choceň, Mr. Pruška. Later I found out that this man had a personal grudge against my father for not accepting him as an apprentice into the factory on account of his low marks at school.

Before leaving Prague I had to deliver letters given to me in London, as at that time the postal service between the countries had not yet been re-established. Our expedition was the first direct one to arrive in Prague after the war. Specifically two deliveries I remember well. One was a letter to the Prime

Minister, Fierlinger, from his sister. I met the Prime Minister at Černínský Palác. There, in appreciation of delivering the letter, I was given royal treatment. The other was a letter to an old lady, Mrs. Penková, at Malá Strana. The letter was from her son, a pilot and the best friend of captain Nedvěd, who'd flown the expedition from London to Plzeň. The mother believed her son was dead. When she learned that the contrary was true, her joy was beyond description. However I was puzzled why she took me for a foreigner until I realized how rusty my native tongue had become after speaking English for six years and using Czech only sporadically.

The train trip from Prague to Choceň was memorable in that the train was so packed it was impossible to exit through the doors at the stations. Instead, one had to climb through the window with the help of other passengers. I was welcomed by our gardener, Mr. Dvořáček, who came to fetch me with a horse cart. The family's automobiles had been stolen by the Russians.

Mother was waiting for me at our villa near her farm, where our family had moved in 1937 from the house next to father's factory. Concern about father's imprisonment outweighed all other emotions accumulated through the six years of our separation. Mother was with Miss Aloisie Urbanová and immediately I learned the details of my father's situation. Then I was introduced to a Russian officer who was billeted in the house at that time. He advised me to collect signatures of people who disagreed with the harsh actions against my father, who were grateful to him for protecting them from the Germans, for employing or providing them with food and coal. According to the officer's experience in the U.S.S.R., once the signatures were delivered to the authorities my father should be released.

My best childhood friend, Jaryna Jeništová-Kutlvašrová, the daughter of my father's foreman and herself an employee of father's factory, who knew practically all the employees, accompanied me on my assignment. During the war father had had about 2,000 employees. Bicycling from door to door all afternoon until late at night we collected hundreds of signatures. I recall that never before or since have I ever been so tired to the extent of throwing up. Finally the list with signatures was in my mother's hands. While resting, I remember hearing voices that later proved to have belonged to two men who came to my mother asking her for the list of signatures with a promise of supplementing them with additional names. We never saw the list again.

Next day I bicycled to Vysoké Mýto where my father was imprisoned. The prison was in the tower on the left side of Mergl's hill. The hill represented a steep access to the town square and a challenge for a cyclist because at that time normal bicycles did not have shift gears. At the top of the hill there was a bicycle shop owned by the father of one of my brother's junior high school classmates. It happened that in front of this shop I met the older son of the shop owner, Jiří Jiráček. He had returned recently from a concentration camp where he was interned on account of his Communist affiliation. On his home-coming, the town council had issued him with the powers of a civil police officer to assist in probing peoples' loyalty to the political regime. Jiří asked me how I was. Not knowing his past or present position I confided in him how I felt, returning home alone after six years, with my brother in the RAF, to find our mother in tears and our father in prison. Jiří consoled me with, "Come tomorrow and I'll see how to help you to get your father out."

Next day after Mr. Josef Dvořáček, our gardener, got the horse cart ready, we set out on our 5-km journey to Vysoké Mýto. Both of us had equally little knowledge of how to master this form of transport but we arrived safely and parked the cart at the back of the tower. Then I went inside through the front gate where I was to meet Jiří Jiráček. When he came we went upstairs to a closed room where my father was brought in. I was so overjoyed to see him that I was not conscious of his discomfort on account of having had his trouser belt and shoe laces removed. It was strange after so many years to encounter a person so high on a pedestal in my own memory who was now so humbled in these circumstances. Yet how insignificant were these thoughts in light of our fears that we might never see him again. Jiří Jiráček left the room with the guards on some pretense, having inconspicuously pointed out to me the back door exit. Once alone with my father, I clasped his hand urging him to move quickly. We ran down the back stairs out of the tower, mounted the carriage, whipped the horses to a fast gallop and in no time our father was once again in mother's arms.

As a novice in a totalitarian regime I lacked fear of the Communists and thus could negotiate with the revolutionary management of the two factories in Choceň and one in Nitra with the help of father's friends. I remember addressing the workers' assembly in the Choceň factory requesting their help to re-establish father's position in the factory. Obviously, I did not succeed.

Because his imprisonment in 1945 was not legal, father was left alone for a while. He started to be interested in farming. I was with him at harvest-time and when the work seemed too strenuous he managed to find a hiding place we could enjoy together, out of sight of the seasoned farm workers.

Later, father established contact with the Minister of Industry, Mr. Laušman, which was followed by a special appointment in Hrádek nad Nisou located in the north of the country. He moved there with my mother and my sister. I stayed behind on the farm. As inexperienced as I was, I tried to manage the farm with the help of Mr. Dvořáček, the faithful gardener. Our first task was to recruit farm hands. In the prevailing chaotic times, most of the workers had left and we had to drive around in the horse cart searching for farm help in the neighbouring villages. My special responsibility was to cook for the non-resident day-time workers. To my surprise they ate very little food. Later I learned that they did not enjoy my cooking, influenced as it was by British Food Guides. My menu included dishes such as cooked beetroot with white sauce, while they would have appreciated dumplings and cabbage.

I found myself in a social environment completely different from that in England, facing the enormous challenges of transition imposed on my parents and my sister's lives. In England during the war people helped and trusted each other. In my country I found that after years of submission enforced through the German occupation, people were distrusting and self-protective. Also, being 21, I was facing the challenges enforced by the prevailing culture in my country – to get married before the age of thirty. In England the age people thought proper for a young woman to marry was higher. I was torn between my wishes to spend time and energy with my parents and my need to safeguard my government employment status, gained in England, which might ensure my basic sustinence. My mother's prayers provided solutions to this dilemma.

9

Life Under Communism

In spite of the problems encountered on the return home to Czechoslovakia, still I felt like I was in a dream – hardly believing I was back in my parents' beautiful villa full of antiques and house plants, on the magnificent estate with its manicured park populated with rare tree species, two ponds and walkway lined with rose bushes. Suddenly we were together again; father released from illegally-imposed internment, mother overjoyed at having back her eldest daughter, and little sister Jarunka, now aged ten, becoming re-acquainted with the big sister she could hardly remember, and with two wonderful helpers, housekeeper Anna, and Josef the gardener. Only my brother Jiří was missing. Mother counted the days till her son would return.

As in prewar days, our extended family got together. There were mother's brother, Dr. Václav Padour, with his charming wife Jarmila and their three boys, my only cousins. I remembered the eldest Václav and his younger brother Jan, but not the youngest Jiří, born during the war. On my father's side there

*Author's mother standing outside house assigned to her
by the Communists, with her grandsons Jiří and Michael*

was his older sister Anežka with her husband Josef Syrový and the younger, good-looking brother Josef, included was great aunt Husarová, the sister of father's deceased mother. To top it all, five days after my arrival, my friend Milada appeared, having travelled from far-away Bratislava with great difficulty caused mainly by the flood of Russian soldiers on all the transport routes. I was overjoyed to see Milada again. How wonderful to see and to touch all these people who were such a big part of my life. How sweet to belong and no longer feel like an alien.

However, the dark political realities had to be faced when, in late 1945, my father was forbidden by the ruling Communist party to enter his factories and when, in 1948, his factories were nationalized. Neither mother nor father were well enough to travel to see our lawyer Dr. Heidrich in Prague and many lawyers in Nitra, Slovakia. And so until my brother's return, I acted on behalf of the family, often accompanied by Milada.

Because our parents' situation was now precarious, it seemed wise to maintain my position at the Ministry of Food, newly established under the Minister Václav Majer from the government-in-exile Ministry of Reconstruction. However, one condition was that I must obtain a Ph.D. degree and in order to be admitted into postgraduate studies, I had first to pass an examination in Czech literature. I received great help from my uncle Syrový, a retired headmaster, and from Mája Malá, the daughter of a good friend of my mother. The examination was held in the antique palace housing the Ministry of Education. There were four of us. My co-examinees were graduates from Yugoslavia.

Having passed the exam, I was free to enrol in the Faculty of Natural Sciences, Department of Anthropology, of Charles University, in Prague. The department specialized in physical anthropology with its research orientation in anthropometry not especially useful for my doctoral thesis in nutritional anthropology. I needed a supervisor with a biological slant. Fortunately Professor Suk accepted me as his last Ph.D. candidate. The disadvantage was that he was located at the Masaryk University in Brno. I had to accept the inconvenience of frequent travels to Brno, about 100 kms from Choceň and 250 kms from Prague. So I entered a period of endless commuting between my home base in Choceň, my employment in Prague, and my thesis supervisor in Brno.

The contact with Professor Suk, Ph.D., M.D., an anthropologist at the University in Brno, was very enjoyable. His research on blood types took him from Alaska to Kashmir and, on my occasional visits to his home, I was fascinated with his authentic portraits of indigenous tribes of Taiwan skull-hunters painted by his brother. Both Professor Suk and his brother were extraordinarily talented people and I was fortunate to have the privilege of their acquaintance.

My Ph.D. convocation was held on June 6th, 1950, in a spectacular hall at the Masaryk University in Brno. There were only three of us, two chemists and myself, receiving degrees. Universities in Czechoslovakia had been closed by the Germans during the occupation, thus completion of post-graduate studies in 1950 was possible for only a few. The two chemists were secondary school teachers whose students gave everyone an enchanting surprise by singing at the finale to celebrate the occasion. I was delighted all my family could share with me this unique experience; it was like a ray of light on the dark skies, in the troubles all of us were going through.

Another happy family memory relates to a few months in 1945. I was working at the Ministry of Food in Prague and my brother Jiří, discharged from the British Royal Air Force, had become a meteorologist at Prague airport. We enjoyed sharing an apartment. An additional joy was when father visited us while in Prague on business. These were very happy occasions for all three of us.

In the summer of 1946 father and Jiří travelled to the United States and Canada to explore future possibilities for starting anew. Apart from the benefit of introducing Jiří to the vast continent, the trip did not affect the future of my father – he did not emigrate, because mother was not happy with the idea of leaving the country. Father and Jiří visited Toronto but the city did not impress father as a provincial capital compared with European cities of similar political significance. I often think what he would say now when I look at the forest of shiny highrise buildings in Toronto, my new home town.

On returning from North America, father became a supervisor in an industrial plant in Hrádek nad Nisou, in the north of Czechoslovakia. He and mother moved there first, followed by my brother and his family. The move turned out to be a disaster, as once again the Communists imprisoned father on false accusations, followed by endless quasi-legal procedures and yet another move for the whole family.

The story was as follows: Originally the plant in Hrádek had been the property of Austrian Jews. It was confiscated by the Nazis in World War Two and used for the production of weapons. After the war the Russians plundered the plant, taking away the machines but leaving behind some industrial material. This material was sold by an USSR Embassy official to my father. Father borrowed the money to pay for the material from his daughter-in-law Milada, my brother's wife and later repaid it. Nevertheless, the Communists accused father of bribing the Soviet official and stealing the material, although it had not been removed. He was imprisoned in Liberec under sad conditions.

As if there could be no end to the disasters, nationalization of all industry by the Communist regime was followed by the dissolution of the farming system. All farmers with property larger than 20 hectares had their land and farm buildings confiscated without compensation. In many cases, the owners were evicted from their homes and forbidden to enter their villages. The confiscated properties were incorporated into newly created co-operatives. This fate applied to the farm of my mother's parents in Vraclav, owned by her brother Václav Padour.

Our farm in Dvořisko was assigned by the Communist regime to the co-operative farming organisation in 1950. In that year my parents' villa had to be evacuated. It was an immense task. Many trucks transported father's antiques, some to the museum in Choceň, most to an antique shop in Prague located on Příkopy, where the objects were displayed in two large halls. The outcome of the sale, mainly to foreigners, was to be the only income for my parents and my sister.

The Communist authorities did allow my parents to keep and move into one of their own one bedroom houses, which father had built for his employees. Fortunately, its location was pleasant, on the banks of the river Tichá Orlice near the park and woods, and not far from the centre of Choceň.

No-one, including my sister Jarunka, was exempted from the harsh impact of Communism. During the war, since the age of six years, Jarunka enjoyed walking from the family villa in Dvořisko, with other village kids, the four kilometres to and from school, trotting through the woods irrespective of the weather. With all the family upheaval, after completing elementary school in 1946 she was placed in Prague in a secondary school call a gymnasium. This was a boarding school, part of a convent of Scholastic Sisters. Suddenly from the freedom of living near the spacious green and neighbouring farms full of animals and life and surrounded by her loving family and friends, Jarunka found herself in what felt to her like a prison. Perhaps her unhappiness contributed to a weakening of her immune system. She was diagnosed with tuberculosis. It took her a whole year to get well. She missed school and moved to live with my parents in Hrádek nad Nisou. When she recovered she returned to Choceň to complete lower secondary school and stayed with the parents of her friend Madla Lustigová. The times were confused under the Communist government. This included the school system. On account of her capitalistic background, Jarunka had no chance of continuing her education in Choceň.

Miraculously, father met in Prague his cousin who belonged to the Communist Party and, because the cousin could maintain a position as a teacher at the School of Fine Art in Prague, he arranged Jarunka's admission to that school. She moved into my apartment where I lived alone since my husband Karel's death in 1949. Also son Jiří, born in 1948, (both events are described in Chapter 10) was being looked after by my mother in Choceň while I worked and studied to qualify for a position at the Ministry of Food.

After our father's release from prison, he was employed as an engineer in a forge near Prague. Thus both my sister and our father shared my apartment. Jarunka and I both enjoyed father's keen sense of humour and his dry wit. We shared the tasks in housekeeping. His ways were totally unorthodox. We found some humour in comparing his ways with those in which we were brought up. For example, he did not adhere to the traditional way of serving food that involved elaborate table settings; in his opinion this required too much dishwashing.

Father was above any pettiness. His spirit soared to higher spheres. He discovered that he had a gift of healing; when he placed his hands on a person who was sick and prayed, the person recovered. He had not been aware of this unusual gift until he himself underwent severe suffering. As this phenomenon occurred at the time when my life was in an utter turmoil I had not registered the change in father, until, some 50 years later, I met in Prague the grand-daughter of a prewar Prime Minister, Antonín Švehla, a friend of my grandfather. To my amazement she recounted how my father's healing had saved her father's life.

While the three of us, father, my sister and I, were living in Prague, little Jiří stayed with his grandmother in Choceň and for a short time had his cousin Madlenka for company. They attended kindergarten together in identical cardigans, knitted by Madlenka's mother Milada.

Those happy days in Prague with my father were too few; this was to be the last year of his life. The temperature in the forge where he was assigned to work affected his health. He was diagnosed with lung cancer and hospitalized in Hradec Králové. Mother and Jarunka spent most of the time with him until he died on August 6, 1953, only 60 years of age.

There we were left behind – mother, myself, my five-year-old son Jiří, my 19-year-old sister and my brother, who was being persecuted for serving as an officer during war in the capitalist British Royal Air Force. Yet, in spite of all difficulties, life had to go on.

Mother continued to care for Jiří after father's death. Jarunka and I commuted by train from Prague to Choceň every weekend to be met at the station by mother and Jiří. On arrival at mother's home, we were often surprised to find baskets of food left at the door by anonymous donors. In those days food was scarce and expensive and these were kind acts of appreciation for mother's past generosity and compassion.

Although, in this period of my life, I discovered the harm that can be caused by human greed and narrow-mindedness, I was fortunate also to discover the spirit of my father, the gift of my child Jiří and the importance of having a sense of mission in life.

Author with our son Jiří and first husband Karel, in 1948

10

My First Marriage

In the summer of 1945 while waiting for a streetcar in Wenceslas Square in Prague I heard a familiar voice, "Hi Madliku". Only Karel Škopek used this nickname. I was not aware that he had already returned from England. As was his usual practice ever since we first met, he started the conversation with, "So, when will you marry me?" It was an old joke. Karel was always joking, always full of spirit.

While working in the Czech broadcasting department I had lived in Ascot with the family of my guardian and commuted to London every day, by taking the bus to Windsor and from there the train to London. On this ride I read diligently the daily newspaper to brush up on the military terms I needed while translating Czech versions of broadcasts. One morning in May 1944 I heard two men sitting by the window talking Czech and I was the subject of their discussion. "Gentlemen, be careful what you are saying, you never know who can understand you", I said in Czech. The better-looking one immediately jumped up, sat next to me and introduced himself as Karel Škopek.

Karel was very sociable, but also mature, much more so than my former friends Tony Jarret and Jiří Honig. Only at the registry office before our marriage did I realise that he was 13 years my senior. With his fair hair and bright smiling blue eyes, so full of life and humour, he appeared much, much younger. No wonder he was very popular among his peers. And importantly to me, my brother liked him as soon as they met. Karel and I dated while in England but we lost touch after I returned to Czechoslovakia.

Karel was born on December 27th, 1911, in Strakonice, a historic town in South Bohemia. His parents, Jan and Albína, had six children. Karel was the youngest. In spite of the family's economic restrictions, Karel's childhood was a happy one. He spent most of his time on the bank of the river Otava, next to their home, where he commanded a whole band of his friends. Sometimes his uncompromising directness caused him difficulties. At school, he defended weaker class mates and fearlessly pointed out any unjustified favours granted by the teachers to their favorites.

Karel was a server and a choirboy in the Catholic church one block from where he lived. At home he played the role of a priest using toy-altars and figures of saints with his older brother John, who later became a monk. Karel also devoted much of his energy to the Scout organization and this influenced his character, in the best sense, in terms of honesty, bravery, love of nature and his place within it, for the rest of his life.

He was the soul of social life not only in the Scouts. At high school, he organized social events and acted in school plays. He succeeded in bringing to Strakonice a famous jazz band with the conductor Mr. Vlach, known as the best in the country.

His mother wished him to be a teacher. Nevertheless,

thanks to his father's moral support, Karel realized his dream, which was to study medicine. This costly enterprise was possible only thanks to his dedicated sister, Anna Hájková, and to her kind husband who lived in Prague. They provided a home for Karel for the many years of his studies. These good people had their own children, twins Libuše and Zdena to look after. The girls were close to their uncle. He often took them to the zoo, as they loved the animals and, in their restricted living quarters in the city, keeping a pet was out of the question.

As a university student Karel used every opportunity to gain experience of countries outside his own homeland; thus as a medic he managed to get residences in hospitals in Austria, Bulgaria, Romania and Poland. In each he easily picked up the respective language and, especially, learned the local songs and sayings. These he used later for entertainment at various social occasions. Karel made many friends in the countries, including Yugoslavia, France and England, thanks to his knowledge of languages and entertainment skills.

Among his many stories was one of his experiences in Poland. Karel accepted a residency in place of a colleague who had declined the position at the last moment. There was no time for Karel to get the required visa. At the border, the custom officer asked pleasantly, "Visa, please." When Karel could not comply with this request, the officer changed his tune and commanded harshly, "Hurry back to Prague, sir!" Without a wink Karel produced a document written in the name of the colleague he was replacing and waving the paper he exclaimed, "Why do I need a visa when I am an official guest of the Polish people?" Thus he managed to enter the country.

At the hospital in Warsaw, he was welcomed joyfully by the local residents. The young men advised him about their national custom of offering a bottle of vodka on first meeting the head of the department. Trustingly, Karel followed their suggestion, bought a bottle of vodka, put it in his pocket and made his way to meet his professor. At the start of the meeting the professor showed delight in welcoming his brother-Slav, a Czechoslovak. All of a sudden his attitude changed and he curtailed the audience with an icy tone by suggesting Karel return to his accommodation. On his way Karel met a nurse who nearly fainted when she saw the bottle in his pocket. "Oh sir, what have you done? Didn't you know the professor is president of the anti-alcoholism league?"

In 1939, before the outbreak of the Second World War, Karel left his homeland fearing German persecution; uncompromising person that he was, he knew he could not live through an enemy occupation. At that time it was practically impossible to leave the country. Crossing the border required a "Durchlasschein" from the Gestapo, the German police. Their offices were thronged by crowds day and night. Although Karel managed, helped by a Czech policeman he was lucky enough to know and who guarded the crowd, to get as far as a German clerk, his request for a permit was denied. Then he tried his luck in Strakonice. He proclaimed with self-assurance that the Prague Gestapo had agreed to give him the permit in his home town. The trick worked. He received a one-month valid permit to work in a hospital in Zagreb, at that time in Yugoslavia.

There he stayed with his friends the Segeti; the father was a former head of a textile factory in Strakonice. As expected, Karel did not return after the month. Such action was considered desertion by the German occupants, for which all of the relatives left behind could be persecuted. Sometimes miracles do occur. There was one decent Gestapo man who sent Karel's identity card to his parents, thus erasing the evidence of his existence. Karel used this case as an example to show that even among evil people there can be an exception – one good man.

In Zagreb, in 1939 Karel met his professor of physiology from Prague who was organizing Czechoslovak expatriates into a group of soldiers. Karel was to assist him and the group was to join a foreign military organization in Syria. At that time Yugoslavia was infested with German spies and organizing such a group was a difficult task. Thus Karel's group pretended to be manual workers from Skoda, the well-known Czech car manufacturer.

During their journey to Syria, the members of the group were dispersed throughout the length of the train. After a while Karel noticed that he was being observed closely by a fellow traveller, a Serbian. After a while, this man addressed Karel, "Where are you employed?" Karel replied as arranged, "I work in the car industry". The man laughed and said, "Looking at your hands, if you're a manual worker then I must be a pope and Mr. Cančik, the Mayor of Přerov (a town in Moravia) is sitting in that compartment over there!" It turned out that the man was not a spy, but an ice-cream vendor for whom the mayor, some years earlier, had signed a business permit. The main trouble was that he wished ardently to join the group, without considering that he had a wife and ten children.

The remainder of the journey produced only disappointment. In Syria their patriotic enthusiasm was cooled by the people they encountered. Many were adventurers rather than patriots. From Syria the group travelled to France and Karel ended up in the town of Agde where the Zagreb group became a part of a disorganized French unit withdrawing before the aggressive German army at the time of the catastrophic Dunkirk retreat. Karel's luck seemed to hold as, just before being captured by the Germans, he managed to get on an over-crowded ship that took him to England. In England, the Czech soldiers were being assembled in Chomley Park in Lancashire. At this point the account of Karel's past is not clear. Why was Karel hospitalized in Birmingham? Was it perhaps because of wounds suffered before embarking on the ship? Later, he was transferred to a centre in Windsor for rehabilitation. There he was released from military service and worked as a medical assistant, commuting every day from Windsor to St. Margaret's Hospital in London where he gained the necessary qualification required to obtain a valid British medical degree, which he did in 1944 from Oxford University. He was fortunate at St. Mary's to work with Dr. Fleming, the inventor of penicillin, the first antibiotic. After graduation, Karel worked as a surgeon in the Emergency Hospital in Dalston, in the east end of London. He stayed there for half a year even after VE Day (Victory in Europe Day – the end of the war against Germany and Italy).

On his return to Prague in August 1945, Karel lived in the accommodation for doctors and nurses within the University Hospital on Karlovo náměstí in the centre of Prague. It was not till after my brother returned from England on September 6, 1946, that Karel visited my family in Choceň.

Karel formally proposed to me shortly after my father's return from his business trip to the USA. The wedding took place on December 7th, 1946. There were many guests. I rejoiced when Marjorie Hayman arrived from England with her four-year-old daughter Elizabeth. My friend Milada was the bridesmaid, paired with my brother, and it was on this occasion that Jiří proposed to her; their wedding was on January 25th, 1947. The other bridesmaid at my wedding was my sister

Jarunka, paired with my brother's school friend Karel Driml. Within two years he emigrated to Australia. All the members of my extended family were present. The merry banquet afterwards was held in my parents' villa. Karel's medical friend Mirek Uher played piano, father played the violin and together they accompanied our guests singing.

The shortage of housing in Prague was horrendous. Forty years later, after the end of the Communist regime, it is difficult to imagine the housing problems that existed in those years. A special permit was required to occupy any housing space. Hardly any new buildings were built. When applying for accommodation in a newly-built house, applicants had to do manual work as volunteers on the building site after their normal working hours. Each person had an allowance of 12 square metres of living space; a tax had to be paid for each extra metre. Of course, the Communist ruling class and the military officials were exempt from these rules.

Large mansions, such as my parents' in Dvořisko, were subdivided and became the home of up to three generations of a family. Another difficulty arose in connection with employment. The labour authority issued work permits to applicants who had to be accepted irrespective of their need of accommodation or the family situation. Thus it happened in many cases that a family had to be split up, mother and children living separately from the father – the breadwinner.

Until June 13, 1947, I was billeted with Karel at the hospital in Prague. We had to share a kitchen and bathroom with other residents. Attempting to get a modern, high-quality apartment with the help of Dr. Hromádko, a lawyer friend of the family, was a great adventure. Originally the apartment belonged to a Jewish family and had been taken over by the Germans during the occupation. After the war, a couple of Czech immigrants from Russia had lived there but the couple divorced and the apartment was empty. Dr. Hromádko was the lawyer processing the divorce. He suggested that we move into the apartment without a permit from the city housing authority. However, the apartment had been already allotted to a Czech officer and one day his soldiers arrived to remove us by force from the apartment. In anticipation of this event, Karel had asked some of his friends who were Air Force officers to be present. Being of higher military rank than the soldiers, they commanded them to leave the premises, against the orders of their superior. Next day, Karel went with a briefcase full of papers to see the official in charge of the case at the city housing department. "These papers document the bribes you have accepted for unlawful assignment of apartments. Do you want me to present them to the higher authorities?" Karel told him. The official paled. Karel's bluff worked and we stayed on in the apartment without official permit, trusting our luck.

Karel and I spent little time together as he was always at the hospital. Sometimes I sat in the emergency operation room just to be able to see him at all. Once I watched him operate on a young boy whose fingers of one hand had been torn off by a grenade explosion. His fingers hung by the skin. Karel sewed on the boy's fingers stitch by stitch, taking hours and hours. In the end the hand was saved. Usually Karel did not talk about his work, but on one occasion he came home very tired, sat down unusually quiet and said, "I can tell by their face whether a person will make it or not." Without sharing with others, Karel knew a lot about life and death.

In the summer of 1947, Karel attended a conference in London and took me along – including watching an operation

on a woman with advanced cervical cancer. The sight of the
damaged tissue and the effect of profuse bleeding were too
horrible. I had to leave the room.

Our best times together were when we travelled to his
native town of Strakonice, to the surrounding region and to
the Šumava mountains. We visited his sister Marie Cvrčková,
who was married to a confectioner in Čkyně and had access
to butter and sugar. Food items were in short supply soon after
the war. Karel knew how to catch trout in mountain streams
with his bare hands and Marie cooked them drowned in
butter. We climbed the mountains, with Karel jumping like a
mountain sheep. I could hardly keep up with him. At that time
we did not fully appreciate the delightful views across the Czech
borders into Austria. One year later, in 1948, a strip of the countryside 20 kms wide was barb-wired and out of bounds.
Czechoslovakia was now in the grip of her Soviet ally.

Karel's work at the hospital ended abruptly. In February
1948, with Soviet backing, the Communists took over the government. Wenceslas Square was the centre of protesters and
Karel positioned himself in a prominent place vehemently proclaiming his disagreement with the coup. His protest inspired
the crowds around him but the next day he was fired from his
post in the hospital. Within two months he found a position as
a general practitioner in the mines located near the small town
of Jílové.

In June 1948, two years after marrying Karel, I was awaiting
the birth of our first child at my parents' villa in Dvořisko, next
to our farm. Karel stayed as long as he could but our son was
taking his time coming into this world. Karel's leave ran out and
he had to return to work. After seeing him off, I also said
farewell to my aunt Jarmila Padourová, who'd bicycled 10 kms

from Vraclav expecting to welcome her first nephew. She'd come one day too soon.

Our son Jiří was born on June 25th, 1948. Our gardener, kind Josef Dvořáček, drove to Choceň to bring the midwife, Božena Daumová, and to alert the family physician, Doctor Lásko. I remember as a child I never wanted to marry a physician because of Dr. Lásko's cold ear – he used to be called to our house when we were sick with scarlet fever or other illnesses with a high fever. This must have been usually in the winter, as I hated the feel of his cold ear on my chest while he listened to my breathing. Stethoscopes were not used at that time. Little did I know that I would marry not one but two physicians.

While Mrs Daumová was heating water in the coal-fuelled boiler, in the bathroom next to the delivery room, Dr. Lásko was having a lively discussion on the subject of Lužičtí Srbové (the Wends). Both my mother and Dr. Lásko were involved in a society interested in this group of people of Slav origin surviving in a sea of Germans. They took no notice of me suffering birth pains. Fortunately Mrs Daumová came out of the bathroom just in time to help the baby into the world. For a number of days before this great occasion my sister Jarunka, aged 13, carried around a gramophone, a rather heavy box as there were no tape players in those days, with the intention of welcoming her first nephew with music. Unfortunately, he appeared when she was fast asleep. However my son was welcomed as a prince. My mother, a connoisseur of artistic needlework, made sure all his little shirts and bed covers were beautifully embroidered with his monogram.

Jiří was one of four children born in 1948 within the circle of our family and friends. The other three were girls. In March, Jaroslava was born to Josef and Anna Dvořáček, our friends and helpers. In April, Madlenka was born to my brother Jiří and his wife Milada. And, in the fall, Pat was born to our friends the Honigs, who were expecting their baby while in the process of emigration to Scotland. Jiří was named after my brother. Madlenka (in full, Mary Magdalene) was named after me; I was named after my grandmother who in turn took the name from her grandmother. Jaroslava Dvořáčková got her name from my sister. Passing on names to the next generation was the usual custom in those days. Who could have imagined then where all these babies would settle in their adult life?

Karel was the happiest father I have ever seen. He did not consider me a very competent parent and except for breast feeding, did most of the nursing when he was around. It was a happy time in Dvořisko, with the three mothers, Milada, Anička and myself, living in close proximity and the proud grandparents watching their first offspring. Jiří was also the apple of the eye of Karel's sister, Anna Hájková, who helped to look after him when we were in Prague.

Karel had to commute to Jilové from Prague. Public transport was slow and cars were scarce. At last he was fortunate to buy an old convertible two-seater Skoda "Popular". He was keen to show it to his parents, Jan and Albina, living in Strakonice. With his sister Anna in the rear seat, and one-year-old Jiří on my lap sitting next to Karel driving, we departed on the morning on September 25, 1949. Drizzling rain was falling, making the asphalt roads slippery. At Nová Hospoda (the New Tavern), near Strakonice, Karel took a sharp turn right. The car turned over.

The next thing I remember was lying on a table in the tavern surrounded by faces; they belonged to the people from a bus that happened to be passing at the time of the accident. My first thought after regaining consciousness was, "Where's little Jiří?" Then I heard his cry and knew that he was alive. When I looked down from the table I saw Karel lying on the floor and cried out in desperation, "Get an ambulance, quick!" A detestable voice replied, "He does not need an ambulance, missus, he needs a hearse". All the rest was a haze. Life seemed unreal and for months afterwards when I saw people on the street my mind turned them into corpses. I could not enter any car.

Everyone, especially Karel's patients, were compassionate and generous and brought gifts, mostly produce from their gardens. Father took care of all the post-mortem procedures. Karel's friend, Mirek Drtina M.D., recommended me to go to the spa of Jeseníky, specializing in the treatment of nervous disorders. Milada, my friend and sister-in-law, accompanied me so that I would not be alone. My parents looked after little Jiří.

My husband Karel was no more. An important chapter in my life had ended abruptly. I was confused, frightened and needing help. In one tragic flash, Karel's son Jiří, a lively toddler, lost his father for whom he never found a substitute. Jiří was loved by all the family, not only because of the tragic loss of his father but also on account of his enquiring mind and unparalleled enthusiasm. These characteristics appealed to his grandfather, Jaroslav Mráz. While for us, his children, father was an authority figure, for his grandson he presented an unexpectedly different image. Jiří spent much of his early childhood with his grandparents in Choceň. When my mother, who suffered from thrombophlebitis, had to be hospitalized for about 10 days, grandfather proved to be an efficient nurse to the little boy. Later on, he was a wonderful play-mate, building model airplanes from scratch, taking Jiří to the airport in Prague and sitting in the cafeteria watching planes take-off, and allowing the four-year-old to taste beer, the Czech national drink. This made Jiří feel important, almost grown-up. My father would be proud to see his grandson's life achievements and to recognize in him many of his own talents, especially the commitment to realize his ideas.

Author with her son Jiří , aged 9, in Prague in 1957

11

Government Researcher

I was fortunate to begin my career in the field of nutrition, an area of interest in any type of political order. *Panem et circenses* – bread and games, the Roman principle for successful governance never goes out of fashion. Socialized agriculture needed experts to develop new food and agricultural policies. These in turn depended on the outcome of food and nutrition research. Thus it became an area of high priority and was well funded.

Thankfully, throughout the difficult and trying years for my family, my research work kept me afloat after my return home from England. Specialists in my area of nutrition were scarce. There was only one very smart colleague with a M.Sc. from the University of Cambridge in England in the nutrition research group at the Ministry of Food. Her area of speciality was bio-chemistry, while mine was anthropology of nutrition, but her principal interest was in politics rather than nutrition. During office hours she was translating Marx's "Capital" from English to Czech and did not join in the work of our food consumption research group. She stayed with the group only a short time before transferring to a newly established Institute of Nutrition with clinical emphasis. The environment there was attuned to her leaning to Communism as the director of the institute was the politically correct Dr. Josef Mašek, M.D.

My experience during the revolution in 1948 is unforgettable. Our office was in the immediate neighbourhood of the Communist headquarters on the Narodní třída, in the centre of Prague. After a night when the Communists with the Soviet backing forced the Social Democrats to merge with them – effectively a putsch that gave the Communists control of the country – I found the head of my department in a state of nervous breakdown. Mr. Toberman was an ardent Social Democrat and strongly opposed to the Communists. "They forced us to merge!" he kept repeating. At my young age, it seemed strange to me to see a man of authority so completely broken in a single night. The same day, all the Ministry's employees were commanded to assemble and vote en masse in favour of the Communist take-over. Only two of us, out of thousands, voted against this. I was protected from the consequences of our action thanks only to the disarray in the administration.

Soon after the Communist take-over, we were joined by Marie Hrubá, a lawyer. She had been a leading figure among the Social Democrats and a candidate for a ministerial post. After the putsch, her political profile was a great disadvantage to her and consequently she was content to be landed in our midst at the Ministry of Food. Marie Hrubá helped greatly in publishing our research work. Oldřich Šmrha was the other member of the group. A graduate of economics, he was skilled at organizing field work, data collection and data processing.

Our team of field workers consisted of about ten young, well-qualified nurses. Education in nursing was close to the discipline of nutrition, which was not an independent academic field at that time in Czechoslovakia. Working with Marie and Oldřich was a great help to me, as I was inexperienced in management and my professional knowledge was raw. As the head of a research group I was the youngest among my peers, the civil servants, mostly older men. In those pre-feminist, bureaucratic times, left over from the rule of the Austrian Empire, male civil servants were not comfortable accepting as an equal a young female arriving from the outside world, influenced by a different culture, and inexperienced in the procedures used in the intra-ministerial communications.

In due course, I, Marie and Oldřich established an excellent research team involved in food consumption surveys. Because of our work we had easy access to large groups of people of different ages, activities and from different geographical areas. And there were no restrictions on the privacy of people's personal information, compared to the Western world.

My work was very challenging. Every morning I went to work apprehensive whether I should be able to manage all the tasks effectively. Evaluating food intake in those days was much more complicated than it is now. Assessing the nutritive value of food intake required the record of all types and amounts of foods consumed in seven consecutive days. Most meals were prepared from scratch as opposed to the ready-made packaged foods which have become so popular in the 21st century. The recipes of the composite dishes and their portions eaten by each subject had to be recorded in great detail. All calculations had to be done by hand, as there were no computers. The work was tedious and subject to errors. Data control was endless.

Our food consumption surveys formed the basis of the nutrition norms issued as directives to caterers providing communal feeding to different groups of population; adolescents, miners, workers in hot environments and in different sports disciplines. The norms served the food inspectors as guides to guard against mismanagement of food by the food providers. Some projects were more interesting than others. For instance, I myself collected data from a team of heavyweight wrestlers. They were extremely kind individuals and during the week of the study, they trained me in their discipline. What an experience. Another time I went along with a competitive team of cyclists involved in the Tour of Warsaw. My professional nutritional guidance on food for the competitors was totally ignored. Each one had his own dietary regime. One cyclist was especially unusual; all his "food energy" came from drinking a special liquid containing alcohol.

The most fascinating research project was shared with a team of endocrinologists. The results were to provide the basis for the iodization of salt to prevent goitre. Population samples were chosen from four different areas of the country. In one mountain region where the staple foods consisted of cabbage and potatoes, people had serious thyroid problems, as cabbage contains thiocyanides, an antithyroid substance blocking the absorption of iodine. In the lowlands, where farmers consumed wheat products, dumplings and dough pastries, they ate an excess of carbohydrates and lacked micronutrients. The best fed people were those in small towns who owned small plots of land where they grew fruits and vegetables for themselves. The women stayed at home and raised hens, rabbits and pigs. The men had a trade or worked in nearby industrial plants. They earned money and could supplement what they grew at home with foods from the market. In the big cities, the problems of nutrition were similar to those experienced by people in wealthy countries in the 21st century – obesity and heart disease.

The results of this survey made me appreciate the African studies of Sir John Boyd Orr describing the impact of nutrition on the stature of two tribes. The Kikuyu, strict vegetarians, were very short. In contrast, the nomadic Masai, living on milk and blood drawn from the jugular vein of the cattle, were tall. Another case of the effect of nutrition on stature concerned Japanese immigrants to the United States, whose change in diet resulted in an increase of several inches in average height over just two generations. These studies not only increased my interest in nutrition, but influenced my area of research in Canada.

In Czechoslovakia under the Communist regime, many of the decision makers who ruled our lives and those who were politically the most influential, lacked even the most basic knowledge in the fields under their jurisdiction, including nutrition. On one occasion I was called to meet with a senior official in charge of a five-year economic plan. He greeted me in high spirits. "Comrade (this was the prescribed title), imagine! According to our food production plans, in five years we expect to produce enough food so that each citizen will be able to consume as much as 7000 Calories every day!" At that time the food ration was about 2000 Calories per day per person. His ignorance made me smile because, at that time of food scarcity, more always meant better, without realizing the public health problems such as obesity, which would be caused by an excessive intake of food. In fact, awareness of food calories among the general public began only half a century later.

While working on food consumption surveys I found the information on the nutrient composition of local foods was not sufficient. Thus one of my projects was to compile a manual of methods for the chemical analysis of items within major food groups. In the 21st century talk about nutrition includes such terms as calories, carbohydrates, proteins and vitamins. When nutrition became my field of expertise, in the 1950s, food was talked about in terms of bread, meat, milk, fruit and vegetables. The translation of food into nutrients has its roots in the second half of the 19th century. First, German chemists Karl von Voit and Rubner analyzed fodder for animals. Later Atwater, an American scientist, applied and developed these techniques to analyze human food which further led to the determination of its nutrient content. In this way, the groundwork was laid giving nutritionists the tools we required to develop standards for healthy diets.

The project involving food analysis required organizing the institutes specialized in research of different types of foods (such as dairy, meat, fruit and vegetables) to analyze the nutrient content of these foods. The composition of milk and eggs varied little as they were already "homogenized" in the respective animal digestive systems from their original energy sources. The challenge came with fruit and vegetables where the variance of nutrient content was great.

This research made me appreciate the impact of soil composition, water and sunlight on the nutrient content, especially of vitamins in plant foods. The feeding regimen affected the composition of meat, eggs and milk. Storage and processing, as would be expected, decreased the content of many of the nutrients on account of oxidation and desiccation in all types of food. Examples of the causes of nutrient variance included the difference in vitamin content; it was high in tomatoes grown at the top of a plant and exposed to plenty of sunshine, compared to low levels in ones shaded by leaves at the bottom of the plant. Politics also had an impact on the nutritive value of foods, for example potatoes. Before Communism, about 60 varieties of potatoes had been available to the farmer. After the collectivization of farming, these were reduced to only 12 varieties chosen for their high yield, as in capitalist countries – their vitamin content was not considered. In the days before the widespread production of synthetic vitamins, such decisions were nutritionally harmful.

My research experience in Czechoslovakia helped me to better understand some of the mysteries of God's Creation. Miraculously, it also provided me with a ticket to an academic career in Canada ten years later.

Author with her co-workers at the car repair shop
in Prague in 1958

12

Troubled Waters

After Karel's death in 1949 I was preoccupied with my employment and academic work at the university, commuting four hours one way from Prague to Brno to my thesis supervisor. At the weekend, Jarunka and I travelled to Choceň, two hours each way, to be with my young son Jiří and our mother. I had to earn a livelihood for myself and Jiří, living with mother. This hectic time lasted until 1950 when I received my Ph.D. Mother needed to keep her house in Choceň, as there was no privacy for her in our Prague apartment. She was only 55 years old when father died and she needed to support herself. To obtain employment she would have to receive a labour permit from the local labour office. And as a capitalist she was allowed only farm labour or child care. Such were the rules. So I implored her to look after Jiří and allow me to contribute to his care.

During this time our research at the Ministry of Food was going well; the food consumption profiles of various population groups, all related to issues significant in the fields of endocrinology, stomatology and high-achieving sports, attracted interest in the field of medicine. Our project into nutrients in food was of interest to the scientists in agriculture and food technology. And finally, the information basic to nutrition guidance and communal feeding programs of various categories of population (ranging from adolescents to the workers in heavy industry) was of interest to specific sections of the government. From our publications, presentations at conferences, and teaching the methodology of our type of research (for example at the Slovakian Institute of Nutrition) I was becoming a well-known member in the Nutrition Society of Czechoslovakia and attracting perhaps more attention than I wanted.

At that time, I was a young, friendly widow around 30 years of age in a world dominated by elder men. Few women held positions at my level. In addition there was a gap of six years when Czech institutions of higher learning had been closed by the Germans, restricting the number of younger people in responsible places. These circumstances exposed me to undue attention from men in positions senior to my own. One example of such interest came in a letter from my boss at the time, a well-known economist, in which he declared that after careful analysis he'd decided he would be better off getting a divorce from his wife and marrying me. Naturally, I was embarrassed; fortunately, just then ongoing reorganisation of the work place moved us apart.

Our research group was located in the same building as the Nutrition Society, directed by Mr. Raboch. In 1952 he approached me, excessively politely, in the manner of the old Austrian bureaucrats, "Comrade Dr. Škopkova, (in

Communism it was compulsory to address people as "comrade" while academic titles were honoured, Škopkova was my married name), would you be so very kind and find time to meet the head of the Department of Medicine in the regional hospital in Ústí nad Labem, Dr. Anthony Krondl? He is conducting research in gastroenterology and is looking for methods of nutrient analysis. I have informed him that you have compiled a manual for this purpose while conducting the project of food composition. Perhaps you could discuss the matter over lunch next time he will be in Prague".

And so it happened. Before I met Dr. Krondl I had his description from those who knew him, as a fine-looking man, rather aloof and equally interested in research as in practising medicine. During the lunch we talked mostly shop. Shortly after this first meeting with Dr. Krondl, a nutrition conference was held in the Mariánské Lázně, which I attended on behalf of the government. Mr. Raboch was in charge of the conference and he invited me to a dinner where Dr. Krondl would be present. Though I found Dr. Krondl interesting, I declined the invitation as I had observed his involvement throughout the conference with one of the attending dieticians, and had decided that he would have little time to talk to other people.

The following year our communication regarding the manual of food analysis was carried on by Dr. Krondl's young doctor-assistant. She informed me that Dr. Krondl was seriously ill with another flare-up of tuberculosis. The first had occurred at the end of the Second World War after he led a medical team during the liberation of the notorious German concentration camp Terezín.

A year later I was surprised to receive a letter from Mariánské Lázně written by Dr. Krondl containing a short message. "I thought of you during the past year of my illness. I shall be in Prague this Saturday. Could you meet me? If not, do write."

From the letter I understood that Dr. Krondl was no longer in Ústí nad Labem and that he was practising medicine in Mariánské Lázně. Was it fate that I went to the suggested meeting? I began calling Dr. Krondl by his Christian name, Tony, and on the following weekends he used to visit me in Prague on his way from Mariánské Lázně to Ústí nad Labem to be with his family, his wife Míla, daughter Milena and son Jan. Our meetings reflected his interest in research; especially I valued his positive comments related to my doctoral thesis. After a year Tony changed his place of work from Mariánské Lázně to Bulovka, a well-known hospital in Prague. He had accommodations in the hospital. Our relationship became close, much to the concern of his and my family and once we realized what was happening we stopped seeing each other. Tony tried to reconcile with his wife, especially in consideration of their children, Milena and Jan; unfortunately with little success.

Tony changed his employment in Prague, accepting a position as head of the clinical department at the Institute of Nutrition, located in Krč, where accommodations for staff were not provided. Housing conditions under Communism were extremely restrictive, so Tony moved into my apartment. My sister Jarunka, still a student, and my eight-year-old son Jiří who'd recently moved to Prague after staying with his grandmother in Choceň, were already living with me. Another occupant was Mrs Anna Chloupková. Her presence deserves an explanation. She was my father's school classmate and one day after he died, I met her on the street. Anna was a former owner of a four-star hotel that had been then confiscated by the Communists. When I met her she was working in a restaurant and could not find accommodation. In our apartment we had a servant's room so I offered it as a temporary solution to her problem. She became a permanent fixture and this was disastrous for my sister because Anna turned out to be a very demanding person who did not appreciate our act of kindness. For over two decades, until her death, Anna was a burden to my sister.

My small apartment became overcrowded. After great effort I managed to find two separate units and so in 1956 Jarunka, with the unfortunate load of Anna, moved into a two-room apartment in Záhřebská Street. Jiří, Tony and I moved into a two-room apartment in Vinařská Street, near the school Jiří was attending since coming to Prague, and where he already had good friends.

Tony's wife sold their house and moved with the children to Prague. The efforts at reconciliation between Tony and his family continued. Understandably, his wife Míla was hurt, deeply offended and worried about the children. Tony was frustrated, as he thought he was going a long way in his efforts to return to the family. In time the discord between husband and wife intensified to such a degree that violence could have occurred.

I felt trapped. Though I loved Tony, my concern for the welfare of Jiří and Tony's children was stronger. I wanted to be disentangled from the whole situation. In the midst of my dilemma in 1956, I received an invitation from Marjorie Hayman, my surrogate mother, to visit her in England. By some miracle I obtained a travel permit and while I was away, my mother looked after Jiří.

What joy it was to be in London with Marjorie and to visit Elizabeth McMaster (née McCaig) and George Honig in Scotland. How free life felt without the burden of the complicated situation back in Prague. Yet, with a heavy heart, I had to return; the Communist authority would not allow Jiří to join me and I could never have left him behind.

While Tony's work at the Institute of Nutrition proceeded well, my own research work deteriorated. Communist oppression grew with the years. Civil servants in my position had to attend courses in Marx-Leninism and the Russian language. There were also frequent administrative reorganizations that caused chaos and affected work ethics.

For a while my own position at the Ministry was not threatened as the recently acquired married name of Škopek distanced me from the family name of Mráz, associated with a capitalist well-known in the small country of Czechoslovakia. I was protected temporarily from political onslaught. However, the Communist machinery did continue to grind slowly and imperceptibly. (In this it differed from the method of control used by fascist dictators, such as Hitler, who persecuted their adversaries with the swiftness of a sword.) Alas, my own luck did not last long and I was soon to be crushed under the Communist boot, like so many others. In April 1958, an anonymous telephone caller asked, "Comrade, what was your maiden name? How many workers did your father employ?" The questions chilled me and immediately I knew what was coming. Government employees were graded according to their family origin and their degree of loyalty to the Communist regime. Members of the Communist Party were in 'A' category. Those loyal to the regime were in the 'B' category. People in 'C' category were allowed to continue in their employment but with no chance of advance. Lastly, persons with capitalist roots, 'D' category, were dismissed and assigned to manual labour.

My grading hearing occurred in front of a special tribunal consisting of regional and local heads of the Communist Party. Five of us who worked in the research institute where I worked were assigned to 'D' category; including, Dr. Fragner, a prominent chemist and pioneer in the manufacturing of antibiotics in the country, and a woman microbiologist whose father was a landowner. The third person later escaped from Czechoslovakia and succeeded as a prominent chemist in Switzerland. The fourth was a librarian whom I met years later in Canada.

I paired with the microbiologist to hunt for a job. We tried to get jobs in construction but gypsies were preferred because they were stronger and we did not succeed. I must admit I found it very hard to look for manual work, since in Europe young people did not have the exposure to odd jobs during their years of study, which is a laudable practice in North America. As a student in England I had been exposed to work in my guardian's factory for about two weeks as part of the war effort, but that had not been enough to earn a living. At the age of 34, I felt completely lost in the world of blue-collar workers.

While searching for a job, I happened to pass by a beautiful lilac bush hiding a dilapidated shack. On closer inspection, I found that it was a car body repair shop and inside I met the manager, a former government economist who'd been sacked for political reasons. He employed me as a car body painter, the only female employee, apart from his secretary. My fellow workers, professionals at their jobs, were all friendly and polite. I especially remember the car body shop store-keeper, an elderly gentleman, and the former owner of a jewellery store.

At coffee-break he used to treat me to excellent coffee in a real china cup and saucer. He was the only person who addressed me formally, in contrast to the others. Back in the 1960s, in Europe, Christian names were used only within the family or among close friends. In other situations people were addressed according to their academic or social standing. I felt uncomfortable when my new co-workers addressed me as "little missus". "With your smile, you'll win big tips from clients," they told me and so one of my tasks became to return repaired cars to their owners. Tips I received went to the head of the working group who used the money to buy beer for everyone. And the beer had to be drunk from a bottle.

What I learned about painting proved useful. My friend and neighbour while living in Podolí, Boženka Novotná, reminds me how on one occasion when she planned to clean window sills I murmured, "Why waste time cleaning, it's so much simpler to paint them." I suspect Boženka regretted losing my painting skills after I returned to a white-collar job.

I worked in the car repair shop for a year, but could not continue there much longer. I had not been trained for it and the environment was hazardous. We worked in a wooden shack with a dirt floor, using acetone to clean car bodies. The fumes of the acetone were pretty toxic. In winter, the rags soaked with acetone were used as fuel in the rickety stoves to heat the shack. It was a miracle no tragedy occurred.

I became too exhausted from the unusual work and found it hard to care diligently for Jiří. The atmosphere at home was not good for any of us, Jiří, Tony, or me. Tony was torn apart with concern for his children, Milena and John. After six years of misery all round, and with no chance of reconciliation between Míla and Tony, the situation was ripe for a divorce.

When called to stand in court, I stated that the family situation was not healthy for Tony's children, or for my own son Jiří or for my adolescent sister living with us.

Tony's divorce was granted in 1959 and it was followed immediately by our marriage at the registry office. (On arrival to Canada ten years later we were married again, first in the Anglican Church and, after Tony achieved the annulment of his first marriage, in the Roman Catholic Church). We moved into an attic, in a somewhat dilapidated villa on a steep hill in Podolí. Though the quality of the living quarters was poor, the attic had an amazingly large balcony overlooking interesting sections of Prague, the river Vltava and the old castle of Vyšehrad.

Once I was expecting a child, I continued at the car shop only for a few months. The work was too heavy. The firm transferred me to another of their branches and assigned me to cleaning offices and workshops. I remember my first experience at the new job. While waiting in the office to be introduced to the shop manager, I overheard the secretaries while they were drinking coffee and smoking, saying, "The office is pretty dirty, high time we had new cleaning staff. There's a rumour the new cleaning woman is some kind of a doctor of science." I piped up, "That person is me!" Happily, the manager decided, after our first meeting, that he could make better use of my time by appointing me his deputy rather than as the cleaning lady. Likely he was satisfied with my work, because he offered me the same position after my maternity leave.

My son Jiří, from my first husband, had to wait 11½ years before gaining a brother, born on January 1st, 1960, a date easy to remember. The birth occurred according to his fathers' orders. Tony took me to the obstetric clinic in Krč; its head was his college chum. In those days, fathers–to-be were not allowed to stay with their wives at the time of delivery so while I was in the hospital Tony took off with Jiří to our cottage in Zadní Třebán. It was located near the home of one of his devoted patients, an elderly lady and an excellent cook, who took good care of both of them.

On my arrival at the hospital, I was told that my doctor, "the Boss", could not be called in until the last few minutes before the delivery, as it was New Year's Eve and he had to celebrate the occasion. While I sat in the waiting room, one by one all the other sighing mothers-to-be were taken to the delivery room until I was the only one left behind. At last a nurse rushed in. "My God, are you still here?" she cried. "You're going to drop the child on the floor!" The delivery took place very soon after my rescue. The "Boss" arrived grumbling. "Where's Tony? I bet he's somewhere drowning his anxiety in beer!" said the doctor, obviously reminiscing of his shared times with Tony in their student days.

When, at last, I was shown my baby I immediately noticed his little bell. My welcome to our new son was, "I hoped so much for a girl." The nurse tried to console me by saying, "We can send him back." Of course I found out later how blessed we were with that good, little child. We named him Michael, after the patron saint of the church in Podolí, where we lived.

Our joy over Michael was clouded with financial worries. I needed money for a washing machine to wash the child's nappies. In 1960, disposable diapers were not available in Czechoslovakia. I was fortunate to get a well-paid contract from a telephone company to develop recipes for their customers. In those days Czechoslovakia traded products of heavy industry with China for soy beans and with the USSR for venison. These foodstuffs were not familiar to Czech consumers. Food was scarce and expensive and so recipes for relatively cheap imported foodstuffs were in demand. In hospital with my new baby, I was surrounded with a small library of cookery books, which I used for inspiration to devise recipes without having a chance to test them. I had to rely on my knowledge and experience in food technology to trust that the dishes would turn out edible and delicious. Fortunately, there were no complaints from my contractor. While I worked most of the day, my neighbour in the hospital room, a young mother from the circles of well-to-do communists spent most of her time with her newborn and with visitors. However, she was not as fortunate as I was. Michael was a good-looking, healthy boy; her little daughter was born with Down's Syndrome.

All patients ate meals in the hospital dining room in two groups; new mothers, and the women who had undergone abortions. The two groups never mixed. I cannot forget the painful and envious glances we received from the other group.

Of course, we were happy because of Michael, but soon saddened by another of the reversals of fortune so common under Communist rule, when my mother's pension was cancelled with the justification that her children should look after her. So I needed money. I could not turn to Tony for help as practically all his salary went to fulfill his obligations to his first family. While Jiří and my mother looked after Michael, I freelanced under a name borrowed from a friend (as I was not allowed intellectual pursuits) and wrote nutrition pamphlets. Still, this was not enough so I tried to sell family jewellery. This had to be done secretly, as officially their origin would be questioned and the items confiscated. The person acting as the intermediary in such a transaction had to be a friend of the family. After I had given my friend the jewels, she told me that the deal had been discovered by the police and that she needed 4000 crowns to pay for legal procedures. The amount represented two to three months' life subsistence to me, yet somehow I managed to borrow the required amount of money from kind people and somehow life went on.

Strangely, I have discovered only 50 years after the fact how my mother's kindness to others during the Second World War helped me to a new occupation. Marie Čamková, daughter of a rich farmer, was conscripted for forced labour in Germany during the war. This regulation applied to every young Czech born in the years 1922 to 1924, in fact the same years of birth as my brother and I. Mother saved many young people from deportation by employing them in father's factory. Later, after the Communist takeover, Marie was smart enough to hide her origins. She became an influential person in Prague's restaurant industry. Thanks to her recommendation, at that time unknown to me, I was offered a job as an assistant manager in a convenience food production unit supplying all outlets in inner Prague. With no experience at all, I had to deal with chefs, butchers, sales persons, all the hygiene requirements and first aid. The job was not always easy. I remember one time when a drunken chef hurt a fellow worker by throwing a knife at her. My boss, comrade Sochor, was a political figure whose main activity was receiving unofficial benefits. With his grade 8 education, it amused him to order me around in front of visitors. One day a teacher from the School of Nutrition, Marie Vinšová, brought her students on a field trip to our plant. Apparently she was amused with my matter-of-fact reaction to the rude manners of my boss. She knew my publications and was surprised to see me in that position.

The experience in the processing of convenience food

gave me a valuable, practical, perspective on nutrition; not to mention the fact that my family appreciated having access to high quality meat, a real treat in a time of meat scarcity.

Next, I was employed as chief technologist at the headquarters of the restaurants and hotels located in the central area of Prague. All businesses were publicly owned and had to comply with many regulations. I learned so much about the inner goings-on in restaurants that to this day, I dine out only as a social obligation. One avenue of activity appealed to me. The Meat Research Institute asked us to devise ways to use meat flaked in a new method of production, rather than ground in the traditional method. The process used sharp projectors shaving thin meat strips and reconstituting the material under pressure into any shape and thickness. I was ordered to set up and organize an experimental kitchen and from this experience, I learned much about the nature of meat.

My involvement with the Meat Research Institute led to a government grant to participate in an International Food Technology Congress held in 1963 in Warsaw, Poland. The trip started with an adventure. At the Prague airport before my departure, I went to greet an acquaintance, the head of food provisioning for airplane passengers and the airport restaurants. He was showing me around with great enthusiasm, when all of a sudden I noticed my plane taking off; I had missed the only way to my destination. However, the manager cooled me down and phoned the dispatcher. The plane returned and landed for me. When I embarked, my fellow passengers were aghast to see an insignificant female boarding the plane instead of the anticipated mighty VIP. This adventure was a testimony to the power of food providers in times of food scarcity.

Warsaw was an amazing place to see, considering that the city was totally destroyed during the Second World War and had been rebuilt as a reprint of the original. The Food Technology Congress was also a landmark in my life. I met two people there, a Finnish food scientist, Sabina Komulainen, and Professor Nell Mondy, from Cornell University, USA. Both were to make all the difference in the world to me as they were soon to be involved in the great changes in our lives that were not far away.

In 1964 I had the opportunity to change my job again. This time it was a teaching post at the School of Nutrition. Time wise, teaching allowed me additional activities such as co-authoring a nutrition textbook and consulting on procedures in a food composition project carried out by the Institute of Nutrition in Prague. Sometimes I walked home along the river Vltava. I felt the love of the river, the city, the people, the country's history; the mismanagement of the country by the Communists hurt me so much that I cried while walking and felt like joining the martyrs who sacrificed their lives for what they believed in – the better future of our fatherland.

In the meantime, my young son Michael advanced from the kindergarten to elementary school and became a favourite of Boženka, my former neighbour in Podolí and her two sons, Tomáš and Pavel. Michael spent so much time at her home that her husband questioned whether he had three rather than two sons.

The family enjoyed a few summer vacations in a small rented cottage in Zadní Třebán, not far from Prague near the river Sázava. Other times we stayed in friends' cottages in the charming Tatra Mountains in Slovakia. During two summers Tony introduced me to canoe trips on the river Nežárka, while Michael was with his grandmother and Jiří with his father Karel's relatives in Sumava.

Jiří had grown into a tall, strong teenager. Yet suddenly

another unexpected blow occurred. In 1965, at the age of 17, he was training for a rowing competition at a kayak club. One day after practice, he hurried home to help us with moving heavy furniture before we decorated the apartment. He had little time, as he wanted to attend a rock concert that evening; his life was a part of the Beatles culture. But instead of hearing Jiří's footsteps, the telephone rang. Tony answered it and paled. Jiří was in the hospital, run over by a truck. "My God! Not another fatal accident in the family," I gasped. Both his thighs had been crushed. Fortunately, the ambulance took him to the best surgeon in the city. Even so, he spent one year in hospital and in the rehabilitation centre before he could walk again. While in the hospital I visited him daily and other family members and friends saw him frequently. Children were not allowed in the hospital, but my sister managed to get Michael in by hiding him under her coat.

Jiří's recovery was incredible. His legs were in one piece again. They regained their strength to such an extent that within five years he could play soccer.

Jiří studied while in the hospital so that he could graduate from the Engineering College with his class. After that, with help of my sister's friends, he was accepted into the School of Architecture. This was his dream – to follow in the footsteps of his much-admired aunt, an architect.

For a while, life seemed to settle down. The rollercoaster seemed to come to a stop, but only for a short intercession.

Author, with mother and sister Jarunka,
shortly before her escape from Czechoslovakia in 1968

13

Escape From Czechoslovakia

After two decades, the tight grip of Communist rule slowly began to loosen. The result was that people became increasingly displeased with the economic exploitation by our Russian "Slav brothers". Our heavy industry and all of our uranium were being sent to the USSR, chiefly for military use, in exchange for "peanuts".

Glints of freedom began to shine as a result of growing contacts with the world outside our national boundaries. Visits by foreign scientists became much more frequent. For instance, Professor Nell Mondy from Cornell University, USA, whom I had previously met at the congress in Warsaw, came to Prague. It was my pleasure to show her around our beautiful city. International meetings started to take place in the country. Tony was in charge of one of them, an International Gastroenterological Congress held in Prague, where he made a number of acquaintances with colleagues from the West, many of whom were helpful to him after our immigration to Canada.

In 1967, it suddenly became easier to obtain permission to travel. I was allowed to travel to Finland on an invitation from the colleague I had met a year earlier at the congress in Warsaw. Starved to see the world, after so many years of confinement in our small country, I took the longest itinerary possible, via East Germany, Belgium, Denmark and Sweden. With almost no money I had to be frugal to the extreme. It was possible to buy the train ticket to Finland in Czech crowns and by travelling at night I was able to save on hotel expenses. I lived on dry sausage and crackers carried from home. The only luxury I could afford was one cup of coffee upon arrival at each of my destinations. I must admit that I also used to drink the whole jug of milk provided as coffee whitener. The money I saved was used to pay for bus tours to learn about the cities I was passing through. Thus I became acquainted briefly with Brussels, Copenhagen and Stockholm. Travelling on a shoestring made me very appreciative of the generosity of my hosts in Finland. Among other experiences, I recall how surprised I was at the use of the sauna by men and women of the family – together and uninhibited by the presence of a stranger. While in Helsinki, at the end of my trip, the film "Dr. Zhivago", describing the revolutionary times in Russia, was in the cinemas. The film was forbidden at home and so I was very keen to see it. I exchanged a gold coin, given to me by my father, which I had brought with me for emergencies, for $60 to buy a ticket to see the picture. All these experiences seem so strange to me now, when travel and films are so easily accessible.

Since his return from England in 1945, my brother Jiří and his family had suffered from the Communists. This was exacerbated by his and his wife Milada's capitalist origins. He took advantage of the relaxed travelling restrictions in 1967 and with his family, including 19-year-old daughter Madlenka and 14-year-old son Jára, they left the country, first to Milada's relatives in Switzerland, then to continue to the USA. As was the norm for families of people who escaped the country, all the relatives' passports were confiscated and this is what happened to my mother, sister and me.

Strangely, this regulation did not apply to my son Jiří, who at that time was 20 years old and a university student. His biological father was not of capitalist descent. He had already spent some time with his follow students during the holidays working in East Germany and in the summer of 1968 he and his friends planned to work in vineyards in the South of France. Thus he had his passport.

The "Prague Spring", the name coined for the awakening of the nation and its inclination to return to its pre-war democratic values, is associated with the name of Dubček, the First Secretary of the Central Bureau of the Communist Party of the Czechoslovak Socialistic Republic. The latter had been the official name of our country since 1953. For my generation, born in the pre-Second World War Czechoslovak Republic, the prospect of change in the regime was too good to be true. And so it proved to be. The Soviets considered the Prague Spring counter-revolutionary. They could not tolerate the risk that they might lose one of their most industrially advanced satellites, if life in Czechoslovakia became more liberal.

In August 1968, Russian soldiers arrived with a terrifying display of force. The night sky was filled with planes, the streets crammed with an endless stream of armed vehicles manned by large, impassive-looking Mongolian soldiers. Yet, not withstanding their massive show of strength, they did not know where they were and Czech people added to their confusion by dismantling or interchanging the signs on roads and streets.

It so happened that, at that very time, I was hosting my Finnish colleague Sabina Komulainen, who had come to Prague on an exchange visit. After so many dreadful historical experiences Finns have an inbuilt terror of their Russian neighbours. My colleague completely lost her nerve. As transport across the city was non-existent, Jiří and I walked her through the chaotic streets to the Finnish embassy. While there, all of a sudden Jiří started considering the possibility of leaving the country and perhaps trying to get to Finland. Our lives were being turned upside down by the Soviet invasion and the political situation pointed to the return of the cruel Stalinist repression of the 1950's.

That evening, my cousin Eva Faltysová and her husband Jan came to consult with me, hoping that my wartime experience as an immigrant in England might help them in their difficult decision whether to leave the country. After they departed, and after my discussion of the bleak prospects for young people in Czechoslovakia, Jiří followed the Faltys with the intention of emigrating with them.

However, overnight Eva and Jan decided against leaving and Jiří returned home. Still, the wheel of destiny was already turning and within less than a week the Faltyses changed their minds and emigrated to Switzerland.

Shortly after that incident, while I was at school teaching a class on the function of the endocrine glands there was a knock on the door. Jiří was with his friend Franta. All he said to me was, "Goodbye mother. We're off to the train station. We're going to Vienna to 'visit' Franta's uncle." Then the two of them left. I went on teaching but not very well. I could barely concentrate on the class and was pre-occupied for the safety of Jiří and his friend. To this day Jiří and I debate how much the Faltyses' decision was critical to his own departure, and subsequently the departure of the rest of his family.

Next day, Franta's step-mother invited Tony and me to visit their home, where we were told of Jiří and Franta's successful arrival at her brother's home in Vienna. From their 6th floor apartment, Franta's father, the deputy Minister of Heavy Industry, made us all look down from the window. "See all those Russian guns down there in the street. All of them were made in our country," he said.

Returning home from this visit, we mounted a streetcar full of Russian soldiers. Tony was extremely upset, and said, "I cannot take this any more, we must leave." His decision was supported by his younger colleague, Pavel Vondrášek, whom Tony arranged to meet in Germany once we managed to get out of the country.

At the time of the Soviet occupation, I was secretary of the union of employees at the School of Nutrition, a social organization with a slight independence from the Communist Party. Any application for a passport had to be endorsed by this union and by the employer. And it had to be accompanied by an invitation from the person at the travel destination. Five students came to me with such invitations, presumably from their "aunts" in Vienna. I managed to get them all the necessary signatures. Later, I met all of them in Vienna and two of them in Canada.

For all the help I was giving the students to leave the country, and for my known anti-communist feelings, I could not expect to maintain my teaching position if I stayed on. At best I might have tried for another job in a car body repair shop, an experience I did not want to repeat.

Tony too was threatened. He was acting director of the Institute Human Nutrition and therefore officially responsible for the anti-Soviet activities of any of its employees. Tony knew that their nationalistic enthusiasm, and his own, would cost him dearly if he remained in the country. Later we learned of the tragic fate of some of the dissident doctors.

Thanks to help from Tony's influential friends, and a faked invitation to visit my colleague's friend in Yugoslavia, we were able to obtain passports not only for ourselves but also for my mother and sister, whom I felt I simply could not leave behind.

On September 15th, 1968, we packed our cases with the essentials. Tony managed to hide a few pieces of jewellery, inherited from my father, in the motor of the car. We picked up eight-year-old Michael from school; he had no idea of our plans. We gave the keys of the apartment to my neighbour and friend, Boženka. She was to pass them on to my cousin Jiří Padour, who for a short time lived in the apartment before being ordered out by the authorities. My sister Jarunka came and gave us all the hard currency she had, about $100. Though Tony and I urged them to come with us, she and mother had decided not to leave. Holding her five-month-old infant Lukáš in her arms, she waved us off bravely. If we did not return, she and our mother would suffer all the consequences.

Leaving my home country for the second time to an unknown destination cannot be compared to my experience of going to England in 1939, when I was 15 year old and accompanied by my brother aged 17. That first trip was arranged by my father. We knew we were expected and would be met by friends. This time was different. I was already 44 years old, my husband was ten years older and we had with us our eight-year-old child. This was not an arranged trip but an escape from anticipated persecution. No-one was expecting us anywhere. We had no clue when or where our journey would end. I did not know how I should manage to find my son Jiří. I was leaving behind the people I deeply loved – my mother, who was without means of support, and my only sister with a five-month-old child. In spite of everything, I trusted the Good Lord and in the end I was not disappointed.

Refugees from Communism:
sons Jiří , aged 20, and Michael, aged 8, in 1968

14

Intermezzo In Vienna

The greatest adventure of our lives had begun. We were cutting off ourselves from our roots for ever (or so we thought), although at that time we did not consider the implications of our decision. Rather, we were overwhelmed with the excitement of getting ready for departure and with the tension connected with safely crossing the border.

The car trip from Prague to the Austrian border took three hours, though to us, filled with fear, it seemed an eternity. The Czech custom officer surprised us with his leniency while searching the car, though he had to be thorough as he was being supervised by a heavily-armed Soviet soldier. At last the gate opened. Tony drove us out of the country we thought we would never see again.

But there was a hitch. Soon as we crossed to the Austrian side of the border and showed our passports to the Austrian immigration officer, he protested, "How come, you have a small boy in your car, but he's not included in your passport? We cannot let him through." In the haste of our departure we had made the terrible blunder of not including Michael on our passports. What to do now? Tony took charge. He telephoned the Austrian Immigration Office in Vienna. Perhaps because he spoke perfect German (his first language as his mother was Austrian) and the fact that he spoke with authority, being used to it in his position and with the aura of his profession, still respected in Europe, he succeeded in convincing officials that Michael should be allowed to come with us.

On arrival in Vienna we intended to search for my paternal aunt Berta, the only relative we had there. I had met her for the first and only time in 1937 while learning German in a Viennese children summer camp. We could not find her. While driving through the streets we stopped and asked two disabled passers-by, maybe because we thought they might be more compassionate than able-bodied people, for advice about where to find a shelter. There were many second-generation Czechs in Vienna who sympathized with the estimated 40,000 refugees leaving the Czechoslovak Soviet Republic at that time, many of them pouring across the Austrian border. Of course, Austrians themselves had had their own experience of Soviet occupation.

Perhaps this is why the disabled gentleman we spoke to on the street directed us to his aunt's hut, or perhaps it should be called a summer cottage. It was located in an area of garden plots in the 14th district of Vienna. These plots were used mainly for growing fruits and vegetables and some of them had huts for storing garden tools and for emergency sleep-overs. Other than access to electricity, these huts had no other utilities yet we considered this arrangement preferable to the official refugee camps, which tended to concentrate human misery. In fact, we were quite happy camping in the garden. By day, we were busy trying to get information. Tony met some of his colleagues in a coffee house in the centre of the city where they exchanged their experiences at different embassies while trying to get visas. We did get visas to England, but after a letter from our friend, Marjorie Hayman, warning us that the English had had enough of immigrants and life would be very difficult, we did not use them.

We also got visas for Germany, but Tony's wartime experience made him uncomfortable at the thought of settling in the country of our former occupiers. Employees at the US embassy were extremely discouraging so we did not apply for American visas. Our last attempt was to try to get visas at the Canadian embassy. Its location was already most inviting and inside we encountered much the kindest employees, compared with those from all the other embassies we visited. After that we did not hesitate where we wanted to immigrate. It was to Canada.

One incident I cannot forget. By chance, I met on the street one of the students for whom I had managed to get signatures, prerequisites for him to obtain a passport and presumably visit his "aunt" in Vienna. When I met him in Vienna he told me of something dreadful that had happened to one of the other students I had helped to get out of Czechoslovakia. The inexperienced student had been lured into some disreputable home and imprisoned there and her passport confiscated. The other students did not know what to do. I took the frightened informant with me to the coffee house where I was meeting Tony and his colleagues. Having heard the frightening story, three of the men immediately got up and, directed by the student, entered the house where the girl was being held. By threatening the owners with the police they rescued the girl, got back her passport and helped her to return home to Prague. The incident made us

124

realize that among the refugees were not only people whose lives and existence were threatened by the Soviet invasion of our country, but also adventurers and naive youngsters taking advantage of the civic disruption.

While trying to live on our meagre means in Vienna, we were advised by experienced refugees not to try to sell anything of value, as the market was already overflowing with goods from other refugees. Instead, they advised us to ask for help from friends outside Austria. After some hesitation we did write for help to three people. They replied promptly, but because of the time it took to exchange letters, their help came only shortly before our departure to Canada. Father's American friend Veselý, from Chicago, sent us $500; my brother, himself very poor after only one year in New York sent us $100, and my friend Dorothy from Quebec also sent us $100. At that time, this was a lot of money and it made us grateful and really appreciate what a treasure it is, when in need, to have real friends. What was even more important, Dorothy in Quebec contacted Dr. McLaren, Dean of the Faculty of Food Science, University of Toronto, after reading about her research work in the newspapers. Dorothy wrote to her describing my research and asking about the possibility of taking me on her staff. The letter must have been well written because I received a telegram in Vienna inviting me for an interview.

To our relief, in Vienna we met Jiří's friend, Franta; he described to us Jiří's departure to England and the news he had from him. We were delighted to learn that apparently Jiří had gone from the airport directly to Marjorie Hayman. This incredible lady had contact with Quakers and through them she acquired financial support for Jiří as well as a job as a drafts-man in an architectural firm and later an admission to the

Architectural Association's School of Architecture, the oldest architectural school in the world.

My younger son Michael was a real help in our situation in Vienna. He immediately became a favourite of our landlady, Mrs Nerad. This lady met regularly with her friends to exchange samples of their culinary art. Michael was a frequent recipient of these delicious samples and generous in sharing them with us.

Michael also had some fun experiences. On one occasion we went to Prater; I believe it is the oldest amusement park in Europe, originally built for the family of the Austrian emperor. We watched the children's train but we could not afford the fare. The driver of the train noticed Michael's longing eyes and invited him to sit next to him. Instead of one ride, as other children would be allowed, Michael spent the whole afternoon on the train.

Once we had our Canadian visas, and even flight tickets given to us by the Embassy (to be paid for later), the car, in which we had arrived from Prague, we left to Franta. He was to hand it over to my cousin Václav Padour, to whom we wrote asking him to drive the car back to Prague, sell it and pay off the bank loan on the car, which was quite a big one. We learned later that all this was accomplished in spite of some difficulties.

As we still had fuel in the reserve jerry-cans in the car, we decided before leaving Europe to drive to Innsbruck, on the invitation of one of Tony's acquaintances, a German doctor who had attended the Congress of Gastroenterology held in Prague in the spring of 1968. When we arrived we were astounded at the reception we received – first class hotel accommodation, a trip to the mountains, special dinner and an introduction to the family – all for poor refugees. At the dinner the host told us, "I must confess to you, I am a former SS officer," he said. This meant that he had belonged to one of Hitler's elite military units, notorious for their savagery and murder. We did not know whether he had a bad conscience about Czechs and wanted to make it up by being kind to us. The situation became very uncomfortable and so, even though we were invited to stay a few more days, politely, and with thanks, we departed.

Our days in old Europe were ending. We were on our way to a totally unknown land far away across the ocean, to a country at once strange and so kind and welcoming to us. We were about to transplant the roots of our forefathers to a new continent. We trusted and we prayed that wherever we went we would be in God's hands.

15

Coming to Canada

Our first transatlantic flight was on October 15, 1968, from Vienna to Montréal in an Air Canada plane with a 100 Czechoslovak refugees as passengers. We arrived in Montréal not knowing what to expect. My geography was poor. All I knew about Canada was that the country was vast. In those days, Canadians knew more about Europe than Europeans about Canada, as many Canadians had their ancestral roots in Europe.

An incredible surprise awaited us when we stepped out of the plane in Quebec. There stood my friend Hanna. She had been the first person who helped me to settle in England in 1939 and here she was again, in a similar situation, after almost 30 years without contact. Both of us had lived through a lot in the time in between, though her story outdid mine. On her return to Prague after the war, only her nanny was still alive. All her own family had perished in Nazi concentration camps. She did not stay in Prague but went to work in the Czechoslovak

Our new home in Toronto

Embassy in Norway. From there she tried to get me out of Czechoslovakia by sending a Norwegian friend to marry me, as she knew how unhappy I was there. Her gesture was kind but not practical. I could not just leave – what about little Jiří, my sister and mother? Still, I appreciated her concern. Hanna herself married Slávek Zuber in Norway and they immigrated to Canada in the 1950s.

In Canada, Hanna was a journalist in the Czechoslovak section of the Canadian Broadcasting Corporation and on account of her position she had a pass allowing her to approach the planes arriving with refugees and to interview them. I had already alerted her from Vienna that we were coming, without giving the exact date and time. So it was big surprise to meet Hanna on the spot. She immediately took us to her home to meet her husband, who instantly got our 100% approval, and after feeding us returned us to the airport to continue on our way to Ottawa, our final destination. Arriving there late at night, the plane was met by members of the local Czechoslovak community. We were driven in a private car to a very decent hotel downtown. These experiences were almost too good to be true after so many anxious days.

One incident stands out in my memory. There were all kinds of people among the refugees; not all of them political refugees, as we were. Specifically one family with two children seemed unusual. The assumed "father" spoke loudly proclaiming himself to be a physician. After hearing him talking, my husband Tony commented, "If that man's a doctor then who am I?" At the Immigration Office, it turned out that the man had no professional documents and it was soon discovered that he was a hospital orderly. That would not have been so important, if his false professional pretences were not the reason why the

assumed "mother" with the children, had come with him to
Canada. Apparently they had met in Yugoslavia while on
holiday and she had been impressed by his social status, which
at that time in Europe commanded great respect. When she
learned of his lies, which happened while all of us were having
lunch in the common dining room, she became hysterical, "You
are a cheat, and I am going to send for my husband." As we
found out later, her legitimate husband happened to be a communist "capo". In return, the "husband" retaliated, "OK, then
I'm going to send for my wife." This pathetically funny case
saddened us all when we realised how the fantastic assistance
from Canadians and our Czechoslovak countrymen was being
misused by some. Fortunately this case was an exception not
the rule.

My first amazement at the differences between Europe
and North America came while shopping. I emphasize I am
referring to the situation in 1968; that is, in the days before glob-
alization. On my first day in Ottawa, the first shop I saw when I
stepped out of the hotel was a mixture of grocery, pharmacy,
post office, stationery and bookshop in one store across the
street. For me, this was unheard of. I was used to shopping for
each type of goods in a separate store. In the old country it was
even illegal to sell baked goods and meat products under one
roof. I was also intrigued to see, in one of the shopping
windows, a real North American Indian outfit. We used to read
with great zeal about the North American Indians; but we
thought they belonged to the world of fiction. Here in one of
the shopping windows, I found evidence that Indians were real
live people.

While staying in Ottawa, Hanna and Slávek Zuber visited
us; they decided that in Canada we needed a car. They gave us

$2,000 cash to buy a Dodge car and ten post-dated cheques of $200 for us to pay them back each month without interest. Within ten months the money was repaid, but our gratitude to our friends for their trust and their caring has remained eternal. Through the Immigration Office, Tony was offered a government position dealing with pharmaceutical legislation. He was grateful, but this was not his world. He longed to continue his career as a clinician and researcher. Not even the ordeal of the written and oral exams demanded from foreign doctors by the College of Canadian Physicians and Surgeons deterred him at the age of 54. It took Tony five years of passing exams to become qualified to specialize in Internal Medicine and be allowed to practice medicine in Ontario. Meanwhile he worked for two years as a resident at St. Michael's Hospital and at the Western Hospital in Toronto and for three years as a senior research fellow at the Clinic for Tropical Medicine and Parasitology at Toronto General Hospital.

Tony and our son Michael were still in Ottawa when I travelled for my interview at the Faculty of Food Sciences at the University of Toronto, located in the Lillian Massey building, on the corner of Bloor and University Avenue across from the Royal Ontario Museum. I carried a briefcase full of my professional credentials and publications. The interview with the Dean, Dr. McLaren, and her assistant, Mrs Armstrong, went smoothly. It was in my favour that I had graduated in England from King's College of Household and Social Science, (renamed Queen Elizabeth College in 1953) and that KCHSS had a mission similar to the Faculty of Food Sciences in Toronto. Both were intended to open up opportunities for women to gain a university education which until then had been restricted to men. My doctorate in anthropology and my research experience were in line with the qualifications they were looking for in the faculty. And I must have spoken English well enough even after 23 years of limited use in Czechoslovakia.

After the interview I was introduced to members of the faculty. Later, I was amused to learn it was not so much my intelligence that helped me in the interview as my outfit. My dear mother had given me US dollars received from father's American friends so that I could buy high quality fabric in one of Prague's special foreign currency only stores for foreigners. With this material I had had an outfit made by the tailor who designed clothes for Mrs. Marta Gottwald, wife of the Communistic President of Czechoslovakia. The tailor came from the same part of the country as my friend Milena Drtinová and myself. Milena recommended me to the tailor, who was an acquaintance of hers. So my job interview was successful and I was given the position of an assistant professor at the University of Toronto, starting November 1, 1968, just two weeks after arriving in Canada at the age of 44.

Looking back, I wonder how many incidents eventually make up our fate. In my case it was escaping from the Germans on my father's decision, studying in England at a college for women, deciding on a career in nutrition, getting a degree in anthropology, escaping from the Communists, benefiting from the contributions of my family's American friends, and appearing at the right time and in the right place, at a Canadian University where new staff with my type of professional background were needed.

16

Toronto the Great City

Both my friends Hanna and Dorothy advised us that Toronto was the best place to settle for English speaking immigrants, and since my appointment at the University of Toronto, it did seem the obvious place to be. As for Tony, thanks to his international medical reputation, he had a recommendation from an English colleague to Dr. K.G.Wightman, head of Toronto General Hospital.

Dr. Wightman and his wife were just about to leave Toronto for a week's conference in the USA. Very kindly he invited us to stay at his house on Glencairn Avenue. Our only responsibility was to feed their cat. If in trouble, we were to contact their friends whose telephone numbers we were given. Oh, the troubles I had. I did not know how to use the can opener for the cat food. So, as instructed, I picked one of the names on the emergency list and called Elisabeth Meanwell. She arrived promptly and opened the can – the cat's life was saved and mine too! Immediately Elisabeth invited me to play tennis with her that

Son Michael with Elisabeth Meanwell

Lillian Massey Building in Toronto

evening at the public tennis court at the end of their street. When I said I had no tennis equipment, she dismissed my objection with, "You can use my husband Harry's shoes and racquet."

Harry Meanwell was head of Parts and Services, Ford Automobile Company, located in Oakville, and one of the kindest men on earth. One incident describes him well. Michael and I went to join Elisabeth and her children at their cottage. Michael and I planned to return to Toronto the same day. Harry arrived at the cottage driving a new sports car with stick shift gears. When he learned that we wanted to leave, he threw his car keys into my lap and told me, "Just leave the car in front of our house." I had not used a car with a gear lever for a decade but somehow I managed to get us back to Toronto in second gear, holding my breath all the way. Such was Harry's faith in people that he did not even question whether or not I could drive.

Harry and Elisabeth were special gifts to the world. Their empathy and their help to those in need was extraordinary. They were also devoted parents, with five children, three of them adopted. Each of the parents were active in the Second World War; Harry on a Naval minesweeper and Elisabeth working as a volunteer military car driver in Halifax. Michael learned his English from Elisabeth and their two daughters, Susan and Mary, who were close to him in age. They opened their home to us and invited Michael on ski trips and to their cottage in Hockley Valley, north of Toronto. We became close friends and for many years Elisabeth used to come downtown practically every week for a shared lunch at the Colonnade, next to the faculty, or at Hart House. We went to seasonal concerts at Massey Hall. Elisabeth was the founder of a book club and she had a vast network of friends. On her recommendation, we sent

Michael to an excellent summer camp, Ponaka, run by one of her friends, Mr Bruno Morawetz, who, interestingly, was also a Czech immigrant.

Michael went to a local school in Toronto not knowing any English. There he met another immigrant boy, Karol Kelen, also from Czechoslovakia, who knew little English but who was only too happy to have a friend who could speak his mother tongue. One of Michael's problems in life was his attitude to food. The baby sitter, to whom he went for lunch, served alternatively canned pasta one day and canned beans the next. To this day, he loathes them both. Often I wonder if this was not the reason why he became, as well as being an artist, both a chef and the author of several books on food.

From the Glencairn house, we moved to an apartment in Thorncliffe Park, on the 16th floor, with a partial view of the lake, recommended to us by the Immigration Office who also gave us $200 to purchase beds, a loan for two months' rent ($270/month) and welfare support. We were astonished at Canadian generosity.

On Canadian Thanksgiving weekend, October 9th,1968, my brother's family arrived in Toronto from New York where they were living. I had warned them on the telephone that we possessed only two twin beds, one for each couple. The children – Michael and my nephew and niece, Jára, age 15 and Madlenka, age 20 – would have to sleep on the floor. Milada, my sister-in-law and also my childhood best friend, describes their trip to Toronto as follows:

"We loaded our second-hand car with inexpensive dishes, blankets, sheets and towels that I had been buying for weeks, knowing from my own recent experience that everything comes in handy in a new household. I added some home-made food and we

set out for Canada in the early morning. It was a gloomy day as we progressed north, and it was raining heavily when we crossed the border via the Peace Bridge. In spite of the miserable weather, our spirits were high and our hearts were filled with joy in anticipation of our reunion. After we found the Krondl's apartment late in the evening and rang the bell, we waited with excitement for the door to open. We heard quick steps and a moment later the miracle of our reunion happened. We hugged and kissed, cried and laughed all at the same time. Our children were happy to see their beloved aunt Madla, uncle Tony and Mike. There was no end to our questions and explanations. We wanted to know everything about them, the family and friends at home in Czechoslovakia, and they had to satisfy their own curiosity about our life. We unpacked the dishes and the food and a real celebration began. We enjoyed our first Thanksgiving Dinner together while standing or sitting on the edge of the bed or on the floor. It was not at all important that there were no chairs. When I observed Madla, I noticed that her ebony black hair was peppered with grey, and that the events of the last year had added a few wrinkles to her face. Still, she radiated happiness. "I feel like a fish in fresh water," she said.

After our move to Thorncliffe Park in November 1969, Tony established contact with the Czechoslovak community in Toronto. Through him, I was invited by the Czechoslovak Women's Club to give a talk on the conditions of women living under Communism. To my surprise, I was greeted there by Mrs Klubalová, who a decade earlier, had also suffered discrimination at the Prague Research Institute at the hands of the Communists. She had arrived in Toronto the year before and was working as a real estate agent. With her assistance, we purchased a house in East York with a loan backed by the

University of Toronto. Our choice was approved by the local borough planner, Sandy McWilliams, a nephew of the McCaig's in Scotland and a fellow harvest worker during the War. It seemed incredible in a city we had hardly heard of, that we found so many friends, both old and new.

My work at the University was challenging, but interesting. I was assigned to teach an undergraduate course, "World Nutrition", close to my earlier area of study in anthropology; in addition, I participated in teaching other undergraduate courses. The research areas in which I became involved, obesity and heart disease, were new to me. These were Dr. McLaren's pet projects. Interestingly, her treatment of obesity became the basis for the procedures of Weight Watcher's. My first graduate students gained some of their materials from subjects in her research. In these projects, I could use my expertise in the methods used in the assessment of nutritional status.

I was also a co-supervisor with Dr. Little from St. Michael's Hospital of a nun Sister Roberta's M.Sc. research project in the area of heart disease. Strangely enough, I came across Sister Roberta 20 years later when she was the head of Providence Villa, where Tony found his final peace in the Wing of Palliative Care .

The University of Toronto's Faculty of Food Sciences had its genesis under the auspices of the Department of Household Sciences, in the building donated by Lillian Massey. With its stained glass windows I felt more like I was in a church than in an academic environment. Here was the beginning of another fruitful chapter in my life. The proximity of the Royal Conservatory of Music to the Lillian Massey Building made it possible to attend lunchtime concerts, which I often enjoyed with our librarian, Miss Betty Newton, an unforgettable English lady. In those days without computers, she would find and duplicate articles from current scientific journals relevant to our areas of teaching and research, and serve them to us on "a silver platter". Sometimes in lunch hours I played tennis on the tennis courts where the Museum of Ceramic Art now stands with Vladimir Miller, a Czech laboratory assistant; in time he became a successful industrialist in the area of food flavours.

The Faculty of Food Science was a socially stimulating place to be. It was the first in Ontario to offer a program for the profession of dietetics, which later transferred to Ryerson University. Also it was much involved with the Toronto Nutrition Committee (TNC), a predecessor of the Program in Community Nutrition, later established in the Faculty of Medicine. The first time Dr. McLaren delegated me to the TNC meeting at Toronto's City Hall, I was much embarrassed, as I was still disoriented in the city and often found it an ordeal just to find my way to the subway. However, shortly afterwards, I was on the editorial committee of the TNC with, among others, Mary McGrath, who was the Toronto Star food columnst for many years.

While the program at the Faculty of Food Science emphasized areas closely related to food and nutrition, some subjects such as design and textiles that had been prominent in the program of the original Faculty of Household Sciences had not as yet been eliminated. One of my life's ambitions was to make my own dress. Dressmaking seemed to me the utmost of skills and I was fortunate under the kind instruction of Professor Betty-Ann Crosby to make my own summer suit. No academic achievement could compare with my pride at this far from simple accomplishment.

And there were other luxuries unheard of by today's staff at the University of Toronto. The faculty had their afternoon tea in a traditional, wood-panelled hall with oak furniture and oil paintings on the wall. We were served fresh-made scones and tea in thin china cups and saucers by the laboratory assistants. How easy it was to develop friendships under such conditions. Especially I remember a young professor, Dr. Colleen Dunkley. Her husband was a well-known organist who volunteered at the Anglican Church St Martin-in-the-Fields, in Toronto. On Colleen's invitation, we were welcomed by the parishioners and the rector of the Church. Michael became an altar boy. For Tony and I, returning to the embrace of a religious community was a spiritual renewal after a long period in the darkness of the atheism imposed by the Communists.

The only shadow in my life was the absence of our loved ones. I dreaded our first Christmas far away from the family – my mother, sister and her son Lukáš left behind in Czechoslovakia. I was tormented by thoughts that they might be persecuted by the Communists because of my and my brother's illegal exits. All my efforts to persuade them to follow us were in vain. I did not worry particularly about my son Jiří who, thanks to his pleasant nature, made friends easily and seemed quite happy to be in England.

We were very pleasantly surprised when Blaženka, the daughter of father's American friend, Mr Veselý, invited us for Christmas in Chicago. It was not easy to go, for new immigrants were not supposed to leave the country for at least six months. However, through the intervention of an Illinois senator smart Blaženka got us a special exemption and permission to travel. The trip to Chicago was unforgettable; we were welcomed with opulent American hospitality and excellent

Czech meals. Blaženka loved to explore her grandmother's Czech traditional Christmas recipes. Michael enjoyed the visit to the zoo. Thanks to their kindness and generous hospitality, we found solace at what would otherwise have been a painful time of the year and a friendship blossomed between our families.

It is good to look back. What often seemed at the time to be coincidence now fills me with awe. The progression of events we experienced was surely more than a series of mere coincidences. Now, it seems clear to me that there is a plan for each of us, directed by the Almighty.

Our last encounter, author with her mother
at Toronto airport in 1971

17

Farewell to My Mother

Three years after we arrived in Canada, my mother came to visit us. Her visit marked a great dividing line between my past life and the future. It was an occasion we had not dared to hope for, an unexpected joy, considering the practical impossibility of her being allowed to leave her country, even for a visit. Somehow she managed to get a visa to the United States to visit my brother and his family. Apparently the Czechoslovak authorities were much less willing to grant a Canadian rather than an American visa. Yet even this obstacle was eventually overcome.

The visit was best described in mother's letter to my cousin Eva Faltysová living in Switzerland. Mother wrote to her in summer 1971, while still in Canada, before she returned to Prague.

"It was a real miracle that I received permission to leave the country. I did not even exert much effort to get it, as it meant a great expense for my children, Jiří and Madla. It happened!

I arrived to New York where I was met by Jiří and his wife Milada and stayed with them on my arrival. I wanted an extension to stay longer but this was refused, with the short comment, "Permission never gets extended". Milada telephoned the Czechoslovak Embassy in Washington and she was told that they could extend the permission for three weeks on condition of receiving a fee of $15. Milada dispatched the money immediately and so I did prolong my stay until August 6th, instead of returning to Czechoslovakia on July 10th. The extra time I hoped to spend in Canada. I received a Canadian visa at the immigration office in Toronto after Jiří and Milada brought me north to Madla's family.

The drive to Toronto from Warren, Pennsylvania, where Jiří's family lives, is a four hour drive. Both families are glad that they live relatively close and can visit a few times in a year. It would have been much further to Toronto from New York City, where Jiří's family lived after coming to the States. My happiness at being with the families was somewhat marred by the thought of what would happen on my return, as the Czechoslovak officials had been so strongly opposed to my going to Canada.

On my arrival in Canada, we were fortunate to be at first with Madla and Michael at the Wightman's cottage at Sauble Beach. Lake Huron is beautiful, with sandy beaches, green groves and attractive cottages. The three of us have a bronzed, healthy colour. I never imagined that in my old age (73 years) I should experience such memorable days. We visited a number of Canadian friends; they impressed me as good people. While I am able to read English without a great problem, speaking it, I have learned to my dismay, is much more difficult than I expected. Fortunately, Mrs. Wightman speaks some French and we have fun when we converse together.

Madla would be very happy if I stayed for good. When I first came to this continent I was very homesick; I did not feel well at all. But now I have settled down and I am not even aware of the fact that I am in Canada, so far away from home. On second thought, no place is like one's own home, though what political harassment, worries over the families of my younger daughter Jarunka and over my sick brother Váša shall I encounter there?

Madla had 2 weeks vacation; after that she had to return to Toronto, as she was teaching a summer course. We were alone with Michael. He was 11 years old and very mature for his age. He was always reading. At school he received a high achievement award. He was especially kind and attentive to me. Madla worried about leaving us alone, so she had invited Zdena Mejta, my niece from Detroit, to come with her little daughter Jana to spend a few days with us.

My grandson Jiří was expected to arrive from London, England, to join us. The night before his departure to Toronto, he hurt his leg and had to be admitted to hospital. In his case, it is very serious, as not long ago he suffered severe injury to both his legs. Madla was beside herself with worry. We got a telegram from Marjorie Hayman that the worst is over, but that he cannot risk a flight to Canada. Madla suggested I should make my return flight to Prague via London to visit Jiří. But I could not do that, I would be very nervous."

At the airport, at the end of mother's visit, I received the most treasured gift of my life and also words that shocked me greatly. Her farewell words, "You are a child I can rely on," were a precious blessing and a gift. But her final words saddened me deeply. She parted with, "I find life very difficult. I am coming to the end." These words were spoken on the 8th of August. Little over four months later, on December 22nd, the telephone rang. My sister, Jarunka, was on the line in tears. "Mother died suddenly of pneumonia after a week in the hospital," she told me. The last rites had been administered by Cardinal Tomášek, a friend of our uncle Váša Padour, the brother of my mother. This was a great comfort to me. The Cardinal was the superior of my cousin Jiří Padour, then a student of theology, who, in due course, became a Roman Catholic bishop. However, when Tony and I were not allowed by the Czech authorities to attend mother's funeral because we were political emigrants, I was devastated. At least her wish to join the spirit of our father was fulfilled.

Only in mature age have I been able to really appreciate what a gift mother was. Her values and her faith created an atmosphere in the home, the place of my childhood, where I spent the most beautiful part of my life, full of light, love, order and discovery.

Thanks to mother, our home was a meeting place for the extended family. Her love and care were reciprocated by all its members. Father could only have achieved his daring plans thanks to mother, and often in spite of her better judgement! Her strength was in her faith. She never complained, even in the most troubled times, after the Second World War stripped of all her possessions by the Communists. She never judged her children's behaviour even if their mistakes caused her sorrow. What a model to follow she was. How fortunate we were to have such a mother.

18

Discovering Canada

I n the small country of Czechoslovakia, there were many
books about adventurers attempting to cross Canada. Many
bright Czech youngsters dreamed of seeing this large and
wonderful land.

The first opportunity Tony and I had to travel came in 1970
and Quebec was the first province outside Ontario that we
visited. Naturally, our first destination was the family of my
college friend, Dorothy Pertuiset-Reed in Arvida. Both Dorothy
and her husband Noel were employed in the Alcan aluminium
plant. At the time of our visit only their youngest daughter,
Elizabeth, was at home. Simone and Marc were both away
at school.

Spending time with the Pertuiset family, at first in their
home and then at their cottage on Lac Saint-Jean, situated in
the neighbourhood of St.Gédéon, not only renewed our friendship, but helped us to view Canada from the perspective of
settlers in Quebec. Up until this visit, our understanding of the

Author with husband Tony and son Michael in Toronto in 1977

differences between Ontario and Quebec had been limited. The first difference we noticed soon as we crossed the border was that roads in Quebec seemed to be in a state of disrepair. The second difference was that it was possible to buy wine in Quebec grocery stores, unlike in "Protestant Ontario". To me, then a very naive newcomer to Canada, it seemed strange to hear everyone speaking French. Throughout our visit, I regretted not having kept up my knowledge of French learned at school; it grieved me that I could not fully appreciate the jolly spirit at Dorothy's parties.

On our return to Ontario, we stopped in the Laurentians Provincial Park, invited there by a couple of Czech immigrants who had arrived with us from Vienna on the same plane. They had secured the position of managers in a newly-built holiday resort in the area, as yet without adequate provision of food and other amenities. We were the only guests, yet our Czech acquaintances did not try to contribute to our wellbeing and so, after a short look at the virgin nature surrounding us, especially at the mountains which reminded us of the Alps (visited just a few years back while fleeing from Europe) we headed home to Toronto. The encounter with the jolly French-speaking Canadians and the vast, empty, beautiful spaces more than compensated for the minor discomfort in the resort.

In the summer of 1973, we were eager to visit the Western provinces. This time we were better prepared for our travels than we had been in the Laurentians. The car was laden with a tent, sleeping bags, heater, lamp, tiny fridge, complete fishing gear and even a canoe strapped to the roof of our green Dodge Dart. We intended to enrich our travelling experience as much as possible, so instead of driving directly north we drove to Tobermory, at the tip of the Bruce Peninsula, and took the old ferry "Norisle" to sail with the car across the short passage to Manitoulin Island. This island was so attractive that we never forgot it and returned there many years later. We drove across the island, then crossed the bridge at Little Current to return to the mainland. We continued through Espanola to our first stop, the national park located north of Lake Superior where we camped for the first time on our adventure. I soon wished it to be the last time. I became the target for so many hundreds of black flies that we had to digress from our route to visit a hospital for treatment. My body was swollen all over.

Travelling through Sault St. Marie and Thunder Bay was quite uneventful. We crossed into Manitoba, leaving Ontario behind, and eventually arrived in Winnipeg. Here we learned a little piece of Canadian history by visiting the Verendrye Monument, dedicated to the celebrated French explorer who camped there in 1742; the University of Manitoba, founded in 1877 and the oldest in western Canada; and the grave of Louis Riel, leader of the Métis in the Red River Uprising against the Federal Government, who was hung on 16th November 1885. Our last visit took us to Fort Garry in the Northern Gateway region to see the remains of a Hudson's Bay Company trading post.

By the time we were in Manitoba I must have acquired immunity to the black fly as we camped in the national parks wherever we could. We were surprised how luxurious and hygienic the camps were, with washrooms, water and firewood. Only occasionally, the camps were overcrowded. At Rushing River National Park, in Manitoba, we encountered a Jehovah's Witness convention with over 40,000 attendees.

Our journey continued into Saskatchewan, where our visit coincided with that of Queen Elizabeth II and Prince Philip attending a centennial celebration of the Royal Canadian Mounted Police. There we noted the British influence in the names of so many people and places. As immigrants from central Europe, so far exposed only to the linguistic difference between Ontario and Quebec, we were impressed by people's respect for the differences in other people's roots and cultures. Along the road in Saskatchewan, we passed a plant processing sodium sulphate. We were astounded at the mineral riches of the country. Further on, we encountered a number of outlets dealing in gems. All of a sudden, Tony was like a child in a candy store as he pored over the great variety of stones, including agates, obsidian, green garnet, tiger-eye, malachite, rhodonite, jasper, aventurine and others. We marvelled at the natural riches of the various Canadian provinces and especially the minerals of Saskatchewan.

In addition to the incredible variety of semi-precious stones, our principal memories of Saskatchewan were of the prairies, which became associated for us with the specific scent of the fields, the songs of the birds and the croaking of frogs. The sounds and smells reminded me of my childhood at our farm in Dvořisko. The animals we saw were of special interest to Michael. In Kinbrook Island Provincial Park, we saw unusually beautiful tiny birds, tame "prairie dogs" similar to chipmunks but even faster moving and more playful, and "prairie chicks", a type of featherless wood grouse. Our journey continued through the southern part of Alberta, where, for the first time, we encountered oil rigs, some of them flaring natural gas. This was in the 1980s when the wasting of precious natural resources was not considered such an issue as it is today.

Our awe at the majesty of Canadian nature continued with the Rocky Mountains, which start in the Yukon and end (as the

Andes) in southern South America, where they contain a
number of volcanoes. Years later, flying over these giant mountains in both in Canada and South America, I shivered at the
thought of the plane crashing into their unforgiving wilderness.
As we drove west, we marvelled at our encounters with Rocky
Mountain sheep, marmots, black bear and, farther north,
grizzly bears, elks and moose.

After the Rocky Mountains, we found ourselves in British
Columbia and, passing Prince George, we continued west
beside the river Skeena. There we had to seek accommodation
far removed from civilization. We found it at the Kispiox
Steelhead Camp where we met Gloria Walker, a teacher by
profession and a colourful individual whose family had originally immigrated to Canada from the Ukraine. Like many other
people living in the North, she had moved up to escape the
rat race prevalent in the South. Each evening, she told us fascinating stories about sharing her life with the Indians who were
her neighbours, which for us was like taking a course in both
Canadian history and sociology. The location of the camp
offered a good opportunity for fishing and Tony caught seven
large trout – a fishing record he never beat!

Our journey westwards ended in Prince Rupert, where we
visited Totem Park, famous for the incredible and majestic
totem poles of the First Nations of the Pacific Northwest. The
spirit and ways of the life of the Indians was well described
in the authentic Indian village of Ksan.

From Prince Rupert we took a ferry to Vancouver Island.
From the ferry we saw water cascading from high rocks to form
mist and create extraordinary effects. We'd enjoyed similar
sights before, while driving below the high rocks beside the
river Skeena. If these waterfalls cannot compete with Niagara
Falls in their volume of water, they certainly did in the beauty of

their natural settings. The sight of them reminded me of my mother's photographs of fjords in Norway. Ever since I saw these pictures I'd dreamed of seeing such sights with my own eyes. Now, decades later, I was seeing them – only they were here in Canada, not in Norway.

Back on firm ground, driving along the Pacific Rim, we had a glimpse of the vast forests, source of Canada's prosperous trade of soft wood, as well as locations of fires, sometimes reaching immense proportions. We camped in Long Beach National Park. How incredible – no flies, just sand, corals and myriads of shells. We cooked our supper on a fire listening to the sound of the sea and in the company of the moon. It was heavenly. Next day we watched, from a rented motor boat, sea lions assembled on the rocks. From afar they resembled a nest of earthworms as they wriggled and turned their snouts up into the air. How they stank and roared! They could be smelled and heard miles away. However, we were compensated by other sights; for example, the varieties of birds flocking around the sea lions enraptured us – and then, to crown it all, a whale blew a short distance from us, letting out a tall plume of water and displaying the magnificent curve of its back as it dived again.

Our trip in the west of Canada offered us the opportunity to visit our friend Dr. Jiřina Vavřik. She had a house in North Vancouver with a view of the Pacific Ocean, and from her we learned more about the life of a Czech immigrant on the west side of Canada. The beauty of the natural environment could seduce anyone to move there. But Eastern Canada also had its advantages. For us, it was nearer to Europe and to our relatives settled in the USA, not so far south of Toronto.

Vancouver was the end point of our journey west. Our return route took us through a real desert. We were astonished to drive miles through a desert (not knowing that such a thing existed in Canada) and then to encounter the "oasis" of Kamloops where soft fruits were growing in the orchards. Since my childhood, and the shortages we experienced during the Second World War, fruits such as peaches and grapes always held great delight for me. I was especially thrilled with the small apricots available there in plentiful supply and not available in Toronto at that time. We stayed with the family of Dr. Novotný, a Czech colleague of Tony, where we received royal treatment, much appreciated on our long journey.

Another unforgettable image of water in its various magical forms was the Athabasca glacier, at the foot of the Columbia Icefield, a dividing line marking the beginning of three rivers; the river Athabasca which later merges with the Mackenzie and flows into the western Arctic Sea; the Saskatchewan river flowing into the Hudson Bay, which connects through the eastern Arctic Sea with the Atlantic Ocean; and the Columbia River, reaching the Pacific Ocean along the west coast of the USA.

Our last stop was Edmonton, Alberta, where we visited the historical museum. In contrast to the peaceful Indians whom we met on our journey, in the museum we saw pictures of Indians ferociously attacking the White Man invading their land.

Our car trip ended in Edmonton on a great note. We telephoned my friend Elisabeth in Toronto to learn that Tony had passed the last of his exams allowing him to practise his speciality of internal medicine. The exams had been a terrible ordeal for him after having been the head of large hospital departments in Czechoslovakia. Yet he accepted that as the price for coming to Canada. Now this good news, capping off our wonderful holiday, was certainly one of life's magic moments.

In Edmonton, after three and a half weeks on the road, we boarded a train to Toronto, thankful for the opportunity to have seen the wonders of nature and learn something about the history of our new land and our fellow citizens. My hope is that these scanty descriptions will serve to whet the appetite of readers not familiar with this vast land – so that perhaps they might follow our footsteps and see the majestic and bountiful nature, which is Canada.

Staff with students in the staff room,
Faculty of Food Sciences, in 1974

19

Teaching as a Twist of Fate

If I had been asked when I was young what I wanted to be when I grew up, becoming a teacher would not have been my answer. Having had the opportunity to learn to fly at an early age, I wanted to become a pilot. In my teens I would have chosen to be a social worker, after having witnessed my mother's involvement in many charitable organizations. I did gain a taste of social work working in the docks area of London during the Second World. However, there I soon discovered that beyond immediate relief, little can be done to help the needy on an individual, long-term basis, and there was not the reward of witnessing the effect of "helping one's neighbour". It seemed to me that social workers were just cogs in large social and political organisations.

My first experience of teaching was in a kindergarten during the Second World War. I remember how touched I was by a very timid boy who always sat apart from the rest of the children. Once, after the class, he handed me a drawing on

the back of a used envelope. From his action, I came to understand how he yearned for love.

After the war, one of my odd jobs in Prague was teaching
nine-year-olds English at an elementary school. I remember
clearly when a shy boy brought me a new edition of an Agatha
Christie mystery novel. On questioning where he got it, I
learned that it had been confiscated from a Western visitor by
his father, a customs officer. Such "unhealthy" books, from
the communist point of view, were not allowed to enter the
country. The father was supposed to destroy the book, not keep
it. The boy brought me the book to please me, without his
father's knowledge; I found teaching the very young was primarily an act of love.

I discovered another aspect of teaching when I taught
youngsters aged 15 to 19 at the School of Nutrition in Prague. I
taught basic science, as well as food and nutrition courses. I had
a Ph.D., but I was specialized in research and lacked teaching
qualifications. Soon, I became painfully aware of this defi-
ciency. Teachers of teenagers clearly require special skills – and
most of these in the gentle art of disciplining.

My first "real" teaching experience, that is to say, the
opening up of minds to different fields of knowledge, was at
the Faculty of Food Science, University of Toronto. The years
1971-1974 saw the beginnings of serious concern about the environment and I participated in teaching an undergraduate
course, "Man and His Environment", with architect Martha
Leitch-Crase and textile designer Betty-Ann Crosbie. At the
advance level, I shared teaching "Food Quality" with Professor
Pat Coleman and Dr. Lilian Thompson, and "Food Service
Administration", together with architect Mr. Keenlyside.

In addition to the regular day-time schedule, most of the

courses were offered at night and in the summer time. For three years, as a service course, I taught medical students in the gastroenterology section.

My main teaching responsibility was the course "World Nutrition". In the early 1970s, with the memory of wartime food shortages still fresh, the idea of under-nourishment was universally understood. Severe food deprivation, leading to starvation and malformation in children, was much less well-known about.

In teaching this course, the task was to bring the concept of the function of food energy out of the metabolic laboratory into the real world; to explain how food energy affects the health, life and performance of human beings. I emphasized the fact that our very existence depends on the nutritional link we have to the earth, the oceans and the sun, and the transformation of this energy from Mother Earth to simple glucose molecules and the priority of the brain as an energy recipient. Mechanisms in our brain maintain the hunger/satiety balance while, at the same time, processing signals of food preferences related to innate taste sensitivity, culturally acquired cues and an individual's beliefs in the health effects of different foods. I stressed the fact that the lack of food energy in the early stage of a child's development stunts both the brain and the body and compromises the immune system, thus facilitating the spread of infection.

Several international charity organizations, such as the Food and Agricultural Organization of the United Nations, tried to alleviate situations of hunger around the world by supplying food to afflicted regions. They soon learned that issues of hunger are often greatly complicated by local social and political conditions. Unfortunately, these have not been resolved, and continue to grow worse to this day. Nevertheless, it was gratifying that some of my students took the issues of food misdistribution to heart and went to work in hunger-afflicted regions overseas. Gradually, I began to appreciate the role of the teacher.

This teaching environment changed drastically at the end of the 1970s when to our sadness, the University of Toronto sold the Lillian Massey Building and discontinued the Faculty of Food Science. Some of the staff, including myself, were transferred to a newly-formed Department of Nutritional Sciences at the Faculty of Medicine. We were no longer a part of an independent academic unit designing its own integrated teaching program leading to professions in food and nutrition. Instead, the new Department offered courses to the huge student body of the Faculty of Arts and Science. From these, only some would choose to major in food and nutrition.

Although my course had to be more general, topics other than malnutrition were covered, such as the rapid development of technology as it affected lifestyle, legislation, and the impact of the food and pharmaceutical industries on nutrition. One area I particularly enjoyed teaching related to food choices at the individual level, including matters of taste and cultural food preferences.

Post-secondary academic institutions give instructors much freedom to design the content and the process of teaching, and allow them to integrate their area of research into course content. This keeps instructors on their toes, by encouraging them to keep up with developments in their field.

One incident left a frustrating memory. After the end of the Cold War in 1992, there was an effort on the part of the international agencies to speed the awareness of the advancement in some disciplines in the countries emerging from behind the Iron Curtain. CIDA (Canadian International Development Agency) invited a French professor from Montréal and myself to go to Prague to design a nutrition course for medical students there. For 14 days and evenings we worked so hard I hardly had time to contact members of my family living in Prague. The understanding was that the generous CIDA grant would be used to bring our work to fruition for the students. It did not happen, and I learned first-hand some of the frustrations connected with foreign aid. Fortunately, this frustration had little to do with the role of a teacher.

The extent of a teacher's responsibility occurred to me when my former student Daisy Lau suggested that I might have "pearls of wisdom" to share. I realized that a teacher, like a parent, not only provides students with specific knowledge, but also offers them a lens through which to observe the world around them and with which to contribute to the development of their own personal value system. This helps students to better understand the ways of the world and this can be both stimulating and enriching for them. As a reward, teachers at the post-secondary level learn about students' systems of values and ways of thinking that may often differ sharply from their own, especially in multicultural environments.

Just like in the parable of the seeds in the Bible, I have seen, over the years, some of my teaching fall on fertile ground. To me, this has been further confirmation that there is no such thing in life as chance, and that if we listen to our inner guiding voice, we can apply our lives in ways that are useful in the world at large.

*Pat Colemen (left) with author in her office in the FitzGerald
Building in 1985*

Daisy Lau, Barbara Floyd with the author in 1982

20

Challenges and Rewards
of Academia

At the time of my engagement at the Faculty of Food
Sciences in 1968 I was not aware the University of Toronto
was in transformation. This was a reflection of the impact on
society as a whole of the rapid advances in technology following the Second World War. In 1970, a drive began towards specialization in many of the University programs. The changes
which affected me directly were made in 1973-1974, when the
Governing Council of the University decided to reorganize
three academic divisions; the Faculty of Food Sciences, the
School of Hygiene and the Faculty of Medicine. The Faculty of
Food Sciences was to be gradually phased out and its undergraduate program transferred to a newly-established program
in the Faculty of Arts and Science. A number of staff from
the Faculty of Food Sciences and from the former Department
of Nutrition of the School of Hygiene were placed in the new
Department of Nutrition and Food Science (later re-named
"Department of Nutritional Sciences"). This unit was established as a basic science department in the Faculty of Medicine.

Each of the components of the new department had a long and respected history at the University. The Faculty of Food Sciences had offered an undergraduate degree program with specialization in nutrition and a graduate program to the Master's level. The School of Hygiene's nutrition unit had operated largely at the graduate level offering M.Sc. and Ph.D. degrees. Over the years, the two units had co-operated in instructing medical students in nutrition, as well as in providing instruction in nutrition for dentistry, nursing, and physical and health education students. The new Department of Nutrition and Food Science offered both graduate and undergraduate programs. In addition, it offered a new Master of Health Science degree (M.H.Sc.) in Community Nutrition.

The period of transformation for these changes to take affect at the University was disturbing, to say the least. The genteel atmosphere of the Faculty of Food Sciences was invaded by a graceless spirit from outside. The faculty's building had been a gift from Lillian Massey Treble. The Faculty of Household Science was the first in the history of the University of Toronto to grant full academic status to women. The founding professors were Annie Laird, directing Household Science, and Dr. Clara Benson, Food Chemistry Department. In July 1978, after a long and successful history serving the University of Toronto and Canada, the Faculty of Food Sciences closed its doors.

The stress of university politics may have contributed to the failing health of Dr. Barbara McLaren, Dean of the Faculty of Food Sciences since its creation in 1962 from the original Faculty of Household Science. Dr. McLaren had arrived at the University of Toronto from Alberta in 1953. I enjoyed working with her for two years before she stepped down as Dean in 1970 for health reasons. Dr. McLaren was a "no nonsense" lady. I felt at ease with her, as she was the same type of person as two of my friends, Elizabeth McCaig, from Scotland, and Canadian Elisabeth Meanwell. Dr. McLaren's friendship was of the type that after work, once or twice she might drop by my office with a suggestion that we go for a drink and a friendly chat at the Park Hotel across the road. Sometimes the drink would be followed by the "chaser".

As Dr. McLaren's health declined, a group of her friends from the University, including Mrs Stauffer, Dr. Alice Turner and Dr. Helen Carpenter, as well as a number of us from the Faculty of Food Sciences, including Professors Pat Coleman, Colleen Dunkley, Violet Currie, the librarian Betty Newton, the Faculty secretary Dolores Olsen and the technician Mrs. A. Gornick, were greatly alarmed by steps being taken by her lawyer at that time. With a power of attorney in his hand, and a lack of relatives to speak for Dr. McLaren, he placed her in St. Raphael Retirement Home, while he himself occupied not only her cottage, but her apartment in Toronto as well. When some of her friends visited Dr. McLaren, she expressed a wish to return to her apartment; the only obstacle seemed to be finding a suitable companion. This could have been overcome by employing Sister Marcella, a nun, whose main objective in life was to help people and who was available. The reaction of the lawyer to this suggestion was unexpected. Instead of welcoming the return of his client to her home, he immediately threatened any "interference" with a judicial injunction. He cited her declining mental faculties as an obstacle to the move, yet at the same time he had her rewrite her will. Dr. McLaren died in 1981 at the age of 71.

The treatment I believe Dr. McLaren received makes me angry even today. At that time I was receiving the kindest treatment from many Canadians and could not believe others could treat their fellow citizen that way. Perhaps I was naive fleeing from communist Czechoslovakia to the paradise that was Canada, or so I believed; I was well used to the cruelties individuals can and did inflict on one another under Communism but it was a shock to see it in Canada.

Without warning in April 1975, and during the upheaval of the transfer of the Faculty of Food Sciences to the Faculty of Medicine, the new Dean of the Faculty of Food Sciences, Professor Iva Armstrong, presented me with a request for the documentation required for my tenure hearing. The request had to be submitted to the tenure committee within one month. In June, 1975, on her last day in the office, Professor Armstrong handed me the denial of my tenure request, with an option to appeal against this decision or to accept a yearly contractual position. One of the arguments for the denial was my age (a touchy issue with women). I decided to appeal. With that in mind, I concluded my letter to the vice-provost and chair of the tenure procedures, Professor Milton Israel, a historian, with the sentence, "Aging females in the primitive societies were not useful as warriors but their counsels saved time and resources, two moieties that are scarce today."

I was granted a tenure-denial-appeal hearing on February 2, 1976, at 8.30 pm, to be held on the 2nd floor of the University College tower. The night was very, very cold and dark, which contributed to an "inquisition"-type atmosphere in the proceedings. But the outcome, received on February 25, 1976, was positive. My tenure appeal was scheduled for March 11, 1976. The letter included even an apology for the denial with an explanation that with the upheaval of the reorganization of the Faculty my documentation had gone astray and had not been received in time for the first tenure committee to consider.

Members of the second tenure committee each received copies of a dossier of my research work in Czechoslovakia and in Canada, including reviews of my work from two outside the University referees. They were Professor Josef Brožek, of Lehigh University, Bethlehem, Pennsylvania, and Dr. Arthur French, of the University of Michigan. In addition there were letters of support from three academicians: R.E. Munn from the World Environment Monitoring System for United Nations, Professor David Anderson from the Department of Mathematics, a member of the Council of the Faculty of Food Sciences, and from Professor Otakar Poupa, from the University of Goteborg, Sweden. The appeal hearing was held in the Faculty of Dentistry, presided over by Dr. G. Nikiforuk. There were nine members of the review committee, among them professors from the University of Toronto's Faculties of Dentistry, Behavioural Sciences, Psychology, Biochemistry, School of Graduate Studies, Department of Nutritional Sciences and a Professor from the University of Guelph.

One question from a member of the committee surprised me, "Why do you have a gap of ten years in your publications while in Czechoslovakia?" The question made me aware, yet again, that many people in Canada's free society had no idea about the political restrictions and persecutions under Communism. A full explanation would have been challenging and time-consuming. I chose a simple answer, "Sir, have you never experienced personal difficulties in your life preventing you from doing what you wanted to do?" I was granted tenure on March 17, 1977, with the status of an associate professorship.

It is difficult to explain my feelings exactly at that time. Canada is such a free, prosperous country, and the expectation of even young people about what they can achieve in their lives is high. So much in this society works to help them, promote and encourage them to grow as human beings, to fulfill, the potential God has created in all of us. Is it possible to imagine exactly the opposite – a country where human characters are broken down, where suspicion exists even between"friends", where one feels trapped as I felt before coming to Canada? In order to live in a free society I was willing to do anything in order to survive. For me, the miracle was that instead of cleaning houses I was allowed to become a professor teaching students.

The location of the new Department of Food and Nutrition was on the third floor of the Fitzgerald Building, at the corner of College Street and University Avenue. At that time, our group was fortunate to be the holder of a considerable grant enabling us to secure two research assistants and a few graduate students. Our research group was accommodated in four rooms. One was a corner room with windows looking out onto Taddle Creek Road on one side and College Street on the other side. We were allowed to take with us pieces of stylish furniture and carpets from the Lillian Massey Building, as the building had to be emptied. I occupied the corner room, also used for consultations. Next were two smaller rooms. One was the domain of Mrs. Pat Coleman, a former Professor at the Faculty of Food Sciences, who opted for part-time university employment because of other commitments; the other room was taken by Mrs. Barbara Floyd, a graduate from the Faculty of Food Sciences and president of a number of women's societies. The fourth room was designated for students and called the "dry laboratory", in contrast to the traditional "wet labs" where chemicals were used. Our group had the best set of rooms in the department; in addition we were fortunate to share a newly-built food preparatory kitchen and a tasting room and we used these in our research projects. Each professor shared half a secretary. At that time, computers were not used for administration, only for special procedures.

My professorial position involved four types of activities and my time was approximately divided as follows: 36% for teaching, 50% for research, 6% for administration, and 8% for such activities as visiting lectures, committee work and scientific meetings. Every year the description of our activities had to be presented to the University administration, on which our "Progress Through the Ranks" was based. My progress to the full professorship ended in 1987, based mainly on the publication of our research findings.

As is evident from the appropriation of time, research was my most important activity. Academic research differs from research in the government, known to me from my work in Czechoslovakia. The latter is used as the basis for government policies, such as dietary guidelines, while the former is attempting to discover, for example, causes of activities such as the choice of foods. The researcher asks not only what people eat, but under circumstances of free choice, why they choose one food over another. This type of research is possible only in an economically affluent and politically stable country such as Canada.

There are many challenges related to launching a research project. All research is costly. Granting agencies have their own bent that has to be considered; thus the research must meet both the academic as well as the practical quest. The study of food choice, for example, first required the design of a conceptual model that would include the physical and psychosocial motives; we called them food perceptions. The next step was the development of an appropriate questionnaire related to individual food perceptions and the choice of a food list. Populations under study differed in age, sex, culture, social condition, and in some projects, condition of health. Statistics, to me, have been always something best avoided, but because they were absolutely essential in my research work I was grateful to have other people available to do them. For example statistical methods had to be used to establish the size of the population sample and to process and evaluate the collected data. The methodology used in this type of research required a sufficiently large population sample to establish meaningful relationships between perceptions of the food chosen and differences within the population. The protocol had to be well tested before its application in the research itself. Field workers had to be well-trained in conducting interviews with the volunteer subjects.

For many years we were fortunate to have the assistance of Daisy Lau in writing requests for research grants. She seemed to have a special talent for anticipating grantors' biases. The cooperation of the population under study was sometimes difficult to secure, especially for long-term projects. In academic research, much of this stage was the students' responsibility, as each project was a major part of their postgraduate degree and their name usually came first when the research was published. Our research group was fortunate to have the cooperation of Mrs. Pat Coleman, not only an excellent researcher but also a gifted writer. Once a project was completed, the last hurdle to be overcome was the process of peer review prior to publication that must be very thorough and can be lengthy.

Many stories can illustrate the problems which may hamper the smooth progress of research. Among others, these may include the personal difficulties of the students, as well as challenges presented by research subjects and the process of the research itself. For example, my student Janice and her boyfriend were ardent spelunkers, a strange sport for most of us. Sometime Janice even practised climbing upwards on highrise buildings, instead of climbing downwards into caves. Tragically, the sport proved fatal to Janice's boyfriend who was killed when he slipped and fell descending into a cave. It took a long time for Janice to get over her loss and as would be expected, the tragedy slowed down the progress of her work. Heroically, she carried on. One winter evening, she called me from a pay-phone in a coffee house where she was working on her thesis, as her dormitory was too cold. She needed help in formulating a certain section of her thesis. As she was writing down what we had agreed on, she shouted, "Oh gosh, my pen's run out, and my pencil is broken. Wait one second, I'll have to use my lipstick to write down the notes." I have never forgotten how many uses a lipstick can have.

Another case illustrates the problems that can be encountered with research subjects. A Ph.D candidate, my student Jennifer, had a very hard time keeping her subjects on a specific diet for six months. On one dark, snowy evening, one subject who lived in Barrie, far from Toronto, consented to an evening interview. Jennifer arrived at her destination, exhausted after the long drive in the dark, only to be refused the interview because the subject said she had to go out to play bridge and had no time.

Part of Daisy Lau's post-graduate project was to develop a model proposing how food choices might be determined according to differing perceptions of a food's physiological effects (its satiating propensity, tolerance and taste) compared to socially-influenced perceptions (familiarity with the food, its prestige value and convenience) and, finally, by its psychological impact (belief in a food's healthiness and a consumer's knowledge of the food's nutritive value). Perceptions of a food depended on the characteristic of the consumers, defined by their heredity, sex, age and physical activity.

In addition, the cultural, societal and economical environment of the decision-maker also had an influence. The description of the model was published in 1975.

In the 1970's, the first attempts to test the model created more questions than answers. The first study was designed to test the impact of the perception of food satiety on food choice among Chinese and Ukrainian women. The second project assessed the impact of three different perceptions of food among low-income women – convenience, price and prestige value. The outcomes of these two studies did not indicate that perceptions of food satiety, convenience price and prestige had a major influence in the process of choosing foods. Even familiarity with foods and knowledge of their nutritive values were not significantly influential. These studies were carried out in the 1970s, before the food industry flooded the market with ready-made foods and before the change of women's role in society. Later studies documented that the major perception affecting food choice was the taste of foods, especially among the young, followed by belief in food's healthiness among older consumers.

I had an opportunity to discuss my interest in perceptions about the taste of food with a geneticist. He recommended that I start my research with taste inheritability. Consequently, he introduced me to Jean Milner, who was in charge of a twin registry at the University of Toronto. In the 1970s, a number of markers were used for differentiating twins. These included placental history, blood grouping and morphological, dermatological and cell properties. At the time DNA was not yet used as a genetic marker. Two groups of young identical and non-identical twins were used to compare taste sensitivity, preference and use of foods between members of each pair. Inheritability among the groups was confirmed with the use of a compound phenylthiocarbamide (PTC), a genetic marker. PTC has a very strong bitter, repulsive taste to those people who can taste it, but no taste at all to some other people, called non-tasters. The sensory difference between the two groups suggested inheritability might be related to preferences and the use of bitter-tasting foods, mainly vegetables of the Cruciferous family, such as cabbage.

This finding prompted another research study to explore whether the genetic trait of sensitivity to PTC has an effect on preference and use of vegetables. We explored the fact that the bitter-tasting vegetables contain goitrin, a substance which is thought to be responsible for the bitter taste of PTC. In the study, four groups of women, pre-menopausal and post-menopausal, PTC tasters and non-tasters were asked to rate the flavour and aroma of cabbage and questioned as to their preference and use of Cruciferous vegetables. The findings of the investigation suggested a minimal genetic effect. Preferences for vegetables of the subjects appeared to be less due to heredity and due more to the consumer's environment. Nevertheless the inherited acuity of taste sensitivity in general cannot be dismissed. Otherwise why would gourmet chefs and pricy gourmet restaurants exist? In fact taste sensitivity is one of the survival mechanisms; hunger being the main one. Sensing bitter taste is considered to provide some animals, including human beings, with some protection from ingesting poison, which usually is bitter-tasting. Preference for sweet taste suggests the brain's desire for a fast energy supply, as sucrose has a shorter metabolic route than other substances. No wonder sweet foods are sought for pleasure, but not vegetables. Experience with food is memorized, evaluated and leads to formulation of food perception in terms of food preference. It is understandable that for older people healthiness of food is more important than to young people. Maintenance of health becomes even more crucial to survival as people age.

An interesting study of the rate of food choice acculturation compared first and second generation immigrant Chinese adolescents and Anglo-Canadian classmates. Second generation Chinese-Canadians showed stronger liking and use of highly processed foods and lower variety of vegetables than first generation immigrants. Second generation Chinese-Canadians demonstrated food preferences similar to those of the Anglo-Canadians. Nevertheless the acculturation was not completed in the second generation. Home influence was the strongest determinant of food use. An impact of culture was explored by comparing combinations of food in mixed dishes among three cultural groups. Women of European and Chinese origin appeared to have more rigid rules for what is an appropriate food combination than women of West Indian origin.

With increasing awareness of the effect of the environment on health there was an upsurge in interest in studying adverse food reactions, also called food sensitivity or intolerance, particularly allergic reactions to food and food ingredients. Two Ph.D. candidates, Sharon Parker and Jennifer Taylor, addressed this issue. Sharon found that most adverse reactions to food are not of immunological origin; rather, other factors, including psychological reactions, were the triggers. Jennifer explored the effect of a very strict diet (Rotary Diversified Diet) in treatments of food sensitivity. Subjects who followed the strict diet, believing in its effect, experienced a decline of the symptoms related to the disease. These two studies provided evidence that psychological factors in treating food sensitivity cannot be ignored. Our work in nutrition behaviour contributed to the methods of marketing products of food by both the pharmaceutical and the health industries. It is rewarding that our study findings contributed to the research in this field; some findings are still being referred to 20 years after their publication.

My last project involved examining acceptability of a special brand of liquid supplements advertised for use by the elderly, in which Pat Coleman, Daisy Lau and I were involved as consultants. The study showed that the nutritional benefits of these products for healthy adults were minimal, but did suggest some improvement in quality of life indices, perhaps due to an increase in folate intake. The involvement of elderly persons in many of our studies led to an interest in our cooperation, first by the Board of Directors of Meals-on-Wheels, Ontario, and later by the Board of Directors of the Ontario Community Service Association (OCSA). The latter was primarily in the hands of Pat Coleman and Daisy Lau.

Officially, I concluded my university career when I retired in May, 1990, with the title of Professor Emeritus. But the work went on. With full administrative departmental support, I continued to supervise my last Ph.D. student until she graduated in 1995. As evident from the Appendix, some papers were published after 1990 as I continued consulting and reviewing grants and journal articles. In 1999 I taught for the last time a course I had originally developed called, "Social and Cultural Aspects of

Nutrition"; sometimes it was taught by Pat Coleman, and after my retirement it was taught by Sharon Parker. I continued to offer visiting lectures up to 2005.

My brief summary cannot possibly reflect all the twists and turns encountered throughout years of doing research. It is hard to believe that projects often involved about a hundred people to design, collect, process and publish the data; and that sometimes 100s of subjects might be involved, some for over six months. Recruitment and continued cooperation of subjects presented many difficulties. The research work was inspiring, but working in cooperation with the students, and especially with Pat Coleman, made all the effort worthwhile.

I appreciated the opportunity to do the type of work that delved into the unknown, tested one's intuitions and opened up new windows in one's mind; the questions asked created new questions. The lesson learned was that one's opinion can never be absolute, but always has to be tested.

21

Travelling in Two Worlds

Confinement within the borders of Communist Czecho-slovakia, before we fled to Canada, left us yearning to see as much of the world as possible. My travels with Tony and Michael and our visits to friends came about mainly from attending professional conferences.

In 1971, our exploration of Canada led us to the Maritimes where the first unforgettable sight in that part of the world was the red earth flower pots on Prince Edward Island.

While driving in New Brunswick and Nova Scotia through the neat villages with their picturesque church towers we almost thought we were back in Europe because the landscape felt so familiar. In 1971, these provinces were known for their prosperous fisheries. No wonder I was able to buy for $1 a crab so huge that I lived on it for three days. Neither Tony nor Michael wanted to share this delicacy; they preferred to avoid unfamiliar foods. Protein concentrates were of great interest to nutritionists in the 1970s and I therefore wanted to visit the fish

Jiří Honig and his wife Dorothy with the author in Scotland in 1986

Tony and author relaxing in Brazil

protein factory being built near Halifax. The structure was never completed, as the abundance of fish dwindled away. From Halifax, we turned north and drove through the vast forest of New Brunswick.

We did not go as far east as Newfoundland while we were exploring the Maritimes in 1971, but Tony and I flew there in 1974 when he was applying for a position at St. John's Hospital. While Tony did his interview, I had time for sightseeing and I was completely overwhelmed with admiration for the beauty of this part of the world. My fascination with Newfoundland was of such proportions that I contacted a local realtor who showed me around. I fell in love with an A-shaped house located on a hill on the other side of St. John's, overlooking a fishing village, from where I could see icebergs and whales. Though Tony's job did not materialize and we did not buy the house, the beauty of Newfoundland has always remained in my dreams.

The last time I visited Newfoundland was in 1984 when I attended an international conference on "Nutrition, Immunity and Illness in the Elderly" held in St. John's to present a paper "Dietary Intake and Food Selection of the Elderly". Among the delegates, there was a prim-looking Japanese scientist travelling with a female companion. The gentleman's English was very limited and as he seemed rather isolated I tried to establish contact by starting a conversation. Pointing to the lady, I asked him, "Is this your wife?" His laconic reply was, "Not wife, student." One evening during the conference all the participants were invited to the local bar to get better acquainted. After consuming some of Newfoundland's "golden elixir" we were granted membership in the Royal Order of Screechers. The ceremony required each of us to kneel, drink a glass of whisky and have a sword laid on one's right shoulder. The

Japanese scientist, although very aloof, felt he had to comply with the procedures. Rarely have I seen anybody more embarrassed than he was on that occasion, especially as he was in the presence of his "student". I was surprised to meet him again in 1985 with the same lady at a conference in Brighton, England. Pleased to see him, I came up and said with delight, "Oh, you and your student!" Again, he gave only the briefest reaction. "Not student, wife," he replied.

I returned to Prince Edward Island in 1982 when I presented a paper, "The Role of Food Perception in Dietary Behaviour of Adolescents", at an international symposium on Adolescent Nutrition and Food Behaviour. During the meeting I established ties with Estelle Reddin, Professor of the University of Prince Edward Island; she asked me to supervise her best student, Jennifer Taylor, during her post-graduate studies. Such was Jennifer's style and energy that she got married just one day after receiving her B.Sc. degree in the summer of 1982 and arrived one day later in Toronto with her new husband. She completed the requirements for her Master of Science degree in 1985 and after some work experience, returned to enrol in a Ph.D. program in Toronto. When she completed this in 1996, she became a professor at her "alma mater" and moved to Charlottetown with two children and her second husband. Jennifer is one example of the amazing young women I have had the privilege to work with at the School of Graduate Studies.

I returned to Halifax in 1986 at the invitation of the dairy industry to participate at a symposium on nutrition and aging. I was to give a lecture entitled, "Can we Modify the Food Habits of Seniors?" I was looking forward to exploring the history of the port of Halifax after my lecture but a strange thing happened. I was well used to giving lectures to hundreds of students, and had, by then, presented papers at many international conferences in my second language English. Yet suddenly, I suffered stage fright – all because my presentation was to be taped. This was my first experience of being visually recorded and the idea unnerved me.

On my way to Halifax, I stopped to visit my friend Dorothy living in a hermitage located in Jailletville, not far from Moncton, New Brunswick. In the past, I had visited Dorothy in many places in Quebec, first in Arvida, then in the Eastern Townships and finally in Quebec City. In 1982, she quit her employment with the Provincial Government of Quebec and decided to adopt the life of a hermit. So there she was, sharing honey from her bees with brown bears, maintaining a simple chapel and working in the newly-established library belonging to the hermits, from which she lent me Thomas Merton's "The Seven Storey Mountain", which greatly influenced my spiritual growth.

Of the many episodes related to my attendance at various conferences in Canada I recall one, at the annual meeting of the Canadian Dietetic Association in 1989, in Victoria, British Columbia, where I was reporting with Daisy Lau on the Meals-on Wheels project. On the table next to the bed in the hotel where we were staying, instead of the obligatory Bible, I found the book, "The Teaching of Buddha", written in Japanese on one page and English on the other. When I asked the hotel manager to sell me a copy of the book, he gave it to me. Reading the book I learned the main ideas presented there were in unison with Christian ideals. Finding the book in the hotel made me aware that Canada was no longer a country only of Christians and that multiculturalism goes hand-in-hand with many faiths.

There were other interesting professionally-related trips within Canada, notably to a gerontology conference in Quebec City in 1986. I was pleased to meet Milada Disman, another presenter of Czech origin, and she has been a dear friend ever since. One encounter is unforgettable. I was trying to find my way to the conference and stopped a couple of young students to ask them in English for directions. When they indicated that they did not understand my English, I repeated the question in my inadequate school French. To my surprise they replied in perfect English. The incident made me appreciate the strength of patriotic sentiments of Quebecers.

My first trip to the USA was in 1970 to attend an international conference on Food and Nutrition in Washington DC. I went especially to meet B.K Watt, joint author of the 1950 edition of "The Composition of American Foods". Her work had been my main reference while working on the composition of local foods in Czechoslovakia from 1952 to 1965. I was surprised also to meet a co-patriot, Pavel Jelen, who was there on a student visa. Very few Czechs were allowed to leave the country under the Communist regime. It was gratifying to meet him later in Edmonton, where he was a professor at the University of Alberta, Faculty of Food Science.

I returned to Washington, D.C. in 1996 to a conference on "The Nutrition of the Elderly" where I was presenting results on the nutritional significance of "Boost", a liquid supplement produced by Mead Johnson. After the conference, Michael arrived from his home in New York City to join me. Visiting the museums and sightseeing around the US capital was doubly pleasurable and memorable in the company of my son, so knowledgeable of art and history.

In Dallas, Texas, in 1980, at a conference on the "Psychobiology of Human Food Selection", Daisy Lau and I presented the paper "Social Determinants in Human Food Selection". While trying to decide where to go for dinner, we met a representative of the conference's sponsor, the Uncle Ben Rice Company. He invited us to a special restaurant where we were served steak, my favourite food. The steak was the size of the whole plate, a full 16 ounce serving. It was the best steak I have ever eaten, but I managed to eat only half of it. Even to this day, I regret having had to leave the other half of that steak on my plate.

In 1983, at the Western Hemisphere Nutrition Conference in Miami, Florida, the topic of our contribution was "Adapting to Cultural Changes in Food Habits". Between sessions, Daisy Lau and I went to have a dip in the ocean and we met an elderly lady apparently feeling lonely and eager to talk to strangers who did not know who she was. It turned out that she travelled regularly between Greece and California and was making a stop in Miami to take a breather. We learned she was a member of the Onassis family and quickly realized that she must know Jacqueline Kennedy, widow of the assassinated American President, John Kennedy. The bits of family gossip she told us would have been a delicacy for the media.

While everybody adores San Francisco, I was out of luck in 1980 when I was there attending a seminar on nutritional anthropology at Berkeley University. I was thrilled to be listening to a presentation by the brilliant Afro-American anthropologist Norge W. Jerome, completely unconscious of her colour, until suddenly taken back by her extreme racist, anti-white position. Coming from Czechoslovakia, where I had seen a coloured person for first time only at the age of 30, I could not relate to her problem. Unfortunately, the discovery of the bitter racial differences in the USA moderated my elation about the content of the seminar and about the natural beauty of San Francisco.

In 1981, I returned once more to California; this time to San Diego, to an international congress of nutrition. Nina Hrboticky, a M.Sc. candidate, Daisy Lau and I were reporting on the findings from our project, "Food Habit Acculturation of Chinese Adolescents". My husband Tony came with us and after the congress, he and I rented a car and drove to Las Vegas. We disliked the place so much on account of the haggard faces of the gamblers that we stayed only one day before taking off to the Grand Canyon. Once there, in the incredible majesty of the place, I came to understand why it is known as one of the Wonders of the World.

The first conference I attended outside Canada and the USA was in Mexico City in 1974. The conference was sponsored by the producers of Bacardi rum and at the welcoming session, held inside a fenced area, there was a bottle of rum on every table, surrounded by opulent dishes of food. Behind the fences, we could see the faces of hungry children; somehow it was possible to pass them some of the food from our overflowing tables. The conference concluded with a performance of Indian and Spanish dances on an improvised stage. It was amusing to watch the shining eyes of the elderly gentlemen scientists tapping their feet in rhythm as the stage floor vibrated under the dancers' feet, specially when they danced flamenco.

My longest trip to an international nutrition conference in South America came in 1978 to Rio de Janeiro, accompanied by Tony. We were part of a group of faculty members and graduate students, including Daisy Lau, from the universities of Toronto, Ottawa, and Montréal and Sherbrook in Quebec. Our adventure started in Colombia when we landed beside the Pacific coast. In the hotel, we were welcomed with the most delicious cup of coffee, tasting more like cream than an ordinary liquid. The highlight of our visit was a visit to a museum displaying unbelievable heaps and heaps of shining gold artefacts. While we were admiring these riches, the guards told us that the gold we were seeing was just a fraction of the treasure shipped from their country to Europe by the Spanish.

Peru was our next stop. We were fortunate to visit Machu Pichu; of course, this is a legendary historical place, yet the impressions of Peru that have stayed with me are more of the innocent, childlike gaze of village people, and the grace of the llamas on the wide-open plains next to the mud huts of their owners.

In Bolivia, unfortunately, the countryside was not safe for tourists. While on the road we were made apprehensive by the anxiety of our bus driver. As we approached any village, he would make certain the doors of the bus were securely closed and drive fast as possible through each village. Seeing the wild crowds, we could understand why. At night, in the hotel in La Pas, we heard shooting and police sirens.

The high altitude made breathing the thin air difficult for some members of our group. We took a boat on Lake Titicaca, the highest lake in the world, where we were given certificates declaring that we had crossed the territory of Manco Kapac, King of the Incas and Lord of the Sacred Lake Titicaca, tasted the sacred water on the Sun Island and received the blessing of the Sun God.

In Argentina, our next destination, we visited a ranch and tasted local foods. In Buenos Aires, we admired the city's incredibly wide avenues and Tony and I danced the tango in the street of its origin.

After visiting the awesome Iguaçu Falls, on the borders of Argentina, Brazil and Paraguay, we at last reached Rio de Janeiro. Unfortunately, I saw little of it. The reason was that my paper at the conference, "Determinants in Food Selection", that had been scheduled originally for ten minutes three weeks earlier, before I left Toronto, had been changed to be among the key presentations and had to last 30 minutes. So while the rest of the party went sight-seeing, I was grounded with Daisy Lau in the hotel extending the presentation.

In Rio, I was elated by the sight of the majestic statue of Christ overlooking the panorama of the city. Other less favourable memories relate, first to the incredible traffic on the city roads in which cars that were less than one inch apart, moved as a solid mass; and second, to the extent of theft. Our hotel, located on the seashore, warned guests to restrict their possessions to only a towel when they went to the beach. So imagine my annoyance when, returning to the shore from a dip in the Atlantic Ocean, I found that even my towel had gone. What a difference from the orderly life we enjoyed so casually in Canada.

We left South America with many strong memories; the majestic Andes, and the contrasts between the dark Pacific coast and the white beaches of Rio de Janeiro, between the heat at the equator and the cool weather of Argentina, between the simple life of Indians – some were descendants of the gentry from Machu Pichu, as well as of the bamboo pipers at Lake Titicaca- and the extraordinary lifestyle of the international society in Rio de Janeiro.

In 1980, Tony and I returned south, this time to Costa Rica in Central America, where he attended a gastroenterological congress. I was fortunate to attend a lecture, dealing with intestinal microbiology. There the thought struck me that human beings are in fact ambulant zoos, with thousands of micro-species living and thriving inside us.

On the return journey, we stopped in Guatemala, where the capital Guatamala City has been rebuilt several times after terrible earthquakes, reminding Tony and myself of the awesome power of nature.

My last long trip with Tony was to western Europe in 1986, during my year of sabbatical leave. Sabbaticals are part of the fringe benefits of being a professor at a university. Professors are exempted from teaching and expected instead to strengthen their academic profile through additional research, publications and academic contacts. A program for a sabbatical has to be approved by the university. For that period of time the salary is reduced. Tony was retired from the university position, but had his own medical practice which he closed for the duration of our travels.

Once in Europe, apart from working, we intended to visit friends, some of whom we had not seen since we fled Czechoslovakia in 1968. Others we had not seen since 1945. In addition, we looked forward to seeing the cultural monuments and places of natural beauty in each region in Europe. Last, but far from least, we were going to attend the wedding of our younger son Michael.

We started our European odyssey at Glasgow airport where we were met by Elizabeth McCaig-McMaster, my wartime school friend at St. Christopher's. I was meeting her husband for the first time but knew Elizabeth's brother and sister, Patrick and Margaret, from my happy summertime visits to their parents' farm in Stranraer, Wigtownshire. Meeting them all was like coming home. We had so much to share. The last time I had seen Elizabeth was after the birth of my son Jiří, in 1948, on her visit to Prague. Since then, she had married Peter and been blessed with three children. Her life had not been simple. The family had shared Peter's brother's farm in Rhodesia (now Zimbabwe) in Africa. When the lives of white settlers there ceased to be safe, they had returned to Scotland. Elizabeth's brother Patrick had inherited their father's farm, Barnultoch, in Stranraer, and Margaret had become a teacher and got married.

We were very pleasantly surprised that our welcoming party included our friends George Honig and his second wife Dorothy who lived in Greenock, not so far from Glasgow. George's first Czech wife had died, leaving him with two children and as a widower he was fortunate to marry again; this time to a real Scottish lady. We stayed with the Honigs in their house overlooking the Firth of Glyde. They took us to the Isle of Bute and then drove us to Stranraer, a place full of some of my best memories during the Second World War. On the route south of Glasgow we passed the Manor Park Hotel which claims that Churchill and Roosevelt met there during the Second World War. From Stranraer, we went to Castle Douglas, the current home of Elizabeth McMaster, her daughters Lindsey, who married a successful farmer, and Sheena, a silver-smith. Peter, Elizabeth's only son, was in the Navy and sailing to Saudi Arabia.

London was our next destination, where we were fortunate to be guests of Marjorie Hayman. Visiting London gave me the opportunity to meet many college friends for the first time since graduation in 1944, including Joan Walsh, Betty Aldridge and Elizabeth Nash and Freda Cowell among others; all of us met at Freda's apartment. Next day, Freda took us to Windsor where I was flooded with many memories of uncle Joe, our kind guardian during the war; he had died in 1946.

We also visited my distant relative Anja Danquith with her children. She lived in London under difficult circumstances, in hiding from her husband who was a medical doctor practising in Ghana. They had married in Prague while he was there on a student visa. Unfortunately she had not anticipated the clash of cultures she would experience when they returned to her husband's homeland. Life had become so bad that she had had to run away with the children and was now living in fear.

On the bright side for us, we enjoyed visiting London's famous historical sites, among them Westminster Abbey and the Tower of London, which I had not seen before, as most of these places had been out of bounds during the war.

The academic program of my sabbatical was to commence at an international nutrition congress in Brighton, on the south coast of England. We stayed in the Old Ship Hotel overlooking the grey sea. Part of the hotel had been blown up by an IRA bomb the week before our visit in an assassination attempt on Margaret Thatcher, British Prime Minister at the time. She survived, the hotel was still open for business and Tony and I enjoyed our stay greatly.

At the congress in Brighton, Tony, who had been director of clinical nutrition at the Institute of Nutrition in Prague before we fled, met a former Czech colleague. Delegates from Communist countries were always under tight surveillance at the international events and had to report all their contacts with "Western" delegates to secret service officials. Tony's former colleague therefore visited us late one night in utmost secrecy. He described for us the tragic fate of the dissidents who had opposed the Soviet invasion of our country in the summer of 1968. One of Tony's colleagues had been stripped of his diploma and, to earn a living in order to have food to eat, had got permission to open up a street stall. Everyday he lived in fear of falling sick; if the stall did not open at the normal hour, official permission would be withdrawn. This could have been Tony's fate if we had not escaped from Communist Czechoslovakia.

For me, the congress also had its professional uses. I met the well-known gerontologist Daphne Roe, who invited me to Cornell University in Ithaca, New York State. I was also reunited with my college friend Louse Davies, the only other person from our year at KCHSS who had followed an academic career; she was renowned for her research in gerontology.

In addition to my own presentation at the congress, "Vegetable Acceptability among Canadian Elderly", both Daisy Lau and Patricia Coleman were also on the program. In the hotel we found Daisy but not Pat. She had not expected a Canadian to need a passport to visit England. Fortunately, she managed to get the right papers at short notice and arrived in time.

After England, our next stop was Amsterdam, in the Netherlands, where we were met by the family of Anja Niewind, a former visiting student working under my supervision. Anja had been sent to Toronto from the University of Wageningen to get exposed to and participate in our type of research. Anja had suffered a terrifying experience while in Toronto and I was relieved to see that she was, at least physically, fully recovered. She had stayed alone, while in Toronto, in the house of a university colleague. One day, after arriving home late at night, she was attacked by an intruder with a knife. Covered in blood, she managed to call an ambulance. The wounds on her head were of such an extent that they required 60 stitches. The police could not find her attacker, but suspected it might have been a patient released from the nearby mental hospital.

We were welcomed by Anja Niewind's current Ph.D. su-pervisor at Wageningen University who arranged for us a stay in the accommodation for guests of the university. In fact, it was a first-class hotel located in a park. Walking in the park before breakfast, we saw many edible mushrooms that, under different circumstances, we would have picked with great delight. A passion for mushroom picking has been with me my whole life – perhaps another blessing of my childhood on our farm.

We visited the Jan Amos Komenský Museum in Naarden, Netherlands. Komenský (1597-1670), a Czech immigrant to the country, was the founder of didactics. His name is known to every Czech child since primary school and we considered it a great privilege to be able to pay homage to his memory at his tomb.

Holland was followed by Germany. We travelled along the river Rhine as far as the Black Forest, stopping at memorable places, before continuing our journey to Switzerland. There we visited my cousin Eva Faltysová, her husband Jan and her mother, my great aunt Marie Kolářová. They lived in Au, near Zurich. From them we learned that the Swiss did not welcome immigrants; quite the contrary to the attitude of people in Canada. The old aunt was not happy in Switzerland. She missed her extended family in Czechoslovakia and, sadly, she died shortly after our visit. We were glad to see the Faltys family – the only relatives in Europe we were allowed to visit. Our family in Czechoslovakia, behind the "Iron Curtain", was to remain out of bounds to us until 1990.

From Switzerland, we drove to Italy on the Via del Sol. Our first stop was Pavia, where I attended an international symposium on "Disorders of Eating Behaviour". Apart from presenting a paper entitled, "The Relation of Body Weight to Alliesthesia", I was asked to chair a session. I came to the lecture room ahead of time to familiarize myself with the environment and to meet my co-chairman, an American whom I had not met before. In the lecture room I met a nicely dressed, very polite gentleman and, thinking he must be my co-chair, talked happily to him, all the time enjoying his smiling face. All of a sudden, an untidily dressed, bully of a man barged in. He, it turned out, was the actual co-chairman; the polite man was a technician who did not understand a word of English.

There was not much time for browsing through the historic city of Pavia. All I managed to achieve was to buy a hat for our son Michael's church wedding before we had to rush down south to San Gimignano where Michael was to marry Maija, his high school sweetheart. The couple had been dating for many years and while travelling in Europe had become so infatuated with San Gimignano that they had promised themselves to have their wedding there. Organizing the event was not an easy task. As foreigners, they had to get all kind of permissions; I myself was involved in getting Canadian documents for Michael. The couple, residents of the US with Canadian citizenship, wishing a ceremony in a Catholic church was not straightforward. In addition, Michael had to reserve a hotel for the family, a country villa for their friends, a restaurant and a car. An added complication was the exclusion of cars inside the walls of the town. All worked out somehow, in spite of all the hassles. The wedding had style and flare, mainly because the couple as well their friends were artists. Spirits were high; some guests even performed ballet in the park next to the town square.

Unfortunately, the bond between the couple did not survive

the geographical distance between Maija's excellent employment in Los Angeles and Michael's artistic need to stay in New York.

From San Gimignano, we went first to Florence, then to Rome and the Vatican and finally to Assisi. In our quick visits, each of these places could give us just a flavour of their treasures and history. In the National Institute in Rome I gave a seminar, "Food Selection in Light of Dietary Compliance". The lecture room was full but, to my dismay during the question period, I found that not all the participants knew English well enough to benefit from the talk.

Driving north again and leaving Italy behind us, we arrived in Vevey, Switzerland, where we were guests of Nestle Ltd. I gave a seminar, "Nutrition and Behaviour in Aging". A Ph.D. graduate from my department, now a researcher at Nestle's, took us to a restaurant high in the mountains, well-known for its "nouvelle cuisine", still fashionable in the culinary world. The secret was that the freshly prepared food was served in 10 courses. Each course was a single mouthful, yet never before or since have I tasted anything so delicious.

My last seminar, "The Role of Taste Perception in the Acceptance of Foods", was given in the Institute for Agrisociology, Department of Psychology and Institute of Nutrition, Justus Liebig University, Giessen, in West Germany. This was the end of the working part of our European adventure.

Before returning to Canada, Tony and I spent a few days of real holidays in Paderborn, West Germany, with our friends Pavel and Luba Vondrášek who we had not seen since 1968 when all of us escaped from Czechoslovakia at the same time. Naturally, each of us had many immigration-related stories to share.

I returned with Tony to Paris, France, in May 1988 for
a conference, "L'Alimentation des Adolescents", organized
by the International Centre for Dairy Documentation and
Information, where I presented a paper on "Food Habits
Determinants of North American Adolescents: Nutritional
Implications". The sponsors of the conference – the French
dairy industry – booked us into a hotel near the Arc
d'Triomphe. Our suite, I remember, had an unusual design in
that the bedroom was located on an open balcony overlooking
the sitting room downstairs. In Paris, we were joined by
Anja Niewind from the Netherlands. We visited Versailles, the
Louvre and the Musée d'Orsai. Although I had been warned
ahead of time, I was still shocked to see a life-size silver statue of
a young string instrument player that was the exact twin of a
statue in my father's house. What a surprise to see a familiar
sight from my childhood in such a different place.

Later in our visit to Paris, we had Pavel Vondrášek from
Germany as our companion and a useful one, on account of his
perfect French. Our sightseeing ended with a visit to the cathedral of Chartres. Especially I appreciated the beauty of Paris
and of the countryside because I could remember visiting with
Karel in 1947, soon after the end of the Second World War, when
the city and the whole country were still recovering from the
damage inflicted by war.

In June 1989, thanks to a grant received the previous
year from the Meals-on-Wheels, Home Support and Senior
Association, I joined a group of about five people (one professor of nutrition from Ryerson University, Toronto, and others
from associated organizations) in an excursion to West
Germany to visit a commercial firm, Apetito, located near the
city of Munster. The firm specialized in food processing and

feeding systems used by Meals-on-Wheels. In addition, we were introduced to various elder-care modules. The German degree of hygiene and efficiency of service were impressive. We learned a lot. One incident amused me there. My companions admired the clean windows we saw everywhere and wondered what type of cleaning fluid was being used; they were somewhat taken back when they found out the admired effect was achieved with elbow grease.

Travel often offers excellent learning experience and by providing general overviews of the field of nutrition, in this regard international conferences were useful. Like many things in life the benefits had to be paid for by the stress of getting grants and other challenges connected with research. Nevertheless, I have been aware that none of the great opportunities that have to come to me would have been possible if I had stayed in Czechoslovakia under Communism.

Perhaps it is difficult to appreciate today, and even more so after the fall of Communism, how much people's lives were ruined, how often their skills and gifts were denied, how rarely people could travel. It has been a blessing for me that I have been able to exercise my intellectual curiosity, and to write, talk and travel freely.

Author celebrating her 70th birthday with
Dorothy Reed and Sr. Marcella Hinz

22

Meeting the Twilight

In 1970, soon after our arrival in Toronto, I met Cyril Gryfe, a Canadian medical doctor, who introduced me to the specialty of geriatrics, the branch of medicine treating all problems peculiar to age and old age. Later, I became acquainted with gerontology, the scientific study of the problems of aging. Dr. Gryfe was leaving for an internship in geriatrics in England, that was not available in Canada at that time. When I expressed surprise over his choice of career, he pointed to the changing composition of the population. His argument was that in the near future there may be as great a need of geriatricians as of paediatricians. Now we see how true his prediction has become.

Our meeting had an effect on me that has lasted more than 30 years and that, in part, directed the course of my professional research. Shortly afterwards, government funds became available for research in various areas of geriatrics and gerontology. In 1978, I received a grant to study nutrition in the elderly and, with my co-workers, we continued in this area even after my retirement. Our research documented the nutritional issues associated with chronic diseases and disabilities among the old, which often require the extensive use of medications. It pointed to the inadequate nutrition of many housebound seniors living alone. One consequence of our findings was that I became involved, mainly with Patricia Coleman and Daisy Lau, in planning and developing standards for Meals-on-Wheels programs. Curiously in all this research, I did not consider how aging might apply to me personally. As a scientist, the aging process always had to be viewed objectively.

How often one's own experience of life differs sharply from our ideas and theories about life. For example, contrary to conventional wisdom, one does not become old suddenly. In my own experience, the aging process has been as gradual as the earlier stages of growing and maturing. Thus, after my retirement, I continued many of my activities and university contacts. Jennifer Taylor continued under my supervision until she finished her Ph.D. thesis. Once retired, I had more time to work on publications, review scientific work, guest lecture and consult to the food industry and community services among others. My busy career as a retired academician – I bear the title of professor emeritus – has offered some unexpected and stimulating challenges. As I have aged, I have been aware of becoming the subject of my own study, of being observed by the professional, academic observer and so I have entered an exciting chapter of self-discovery.

These sunset years have also had dark clouds. My own personal process of aging was affected by my grief over the illness and death of my husband Tony. After a renal failure, and despite a death sentence pronounced by his medical colleagues, he survived on dialysis for another five years. At the very end of his life, spending the last 10 days and nights with him in a room with four other dying persons at the palliative care division of the Providence Centre Villa, I became intimate with the change of the sound of breathing as a person dies.

In the days following Tony's death I remained in a state of perpetual daze. Family and friends were compassionate as, for the second time, I joined the ranks of the millions of widows. After the shock, came a time of having to learn how to live alone. The effort to maintain emotional, intellectual, spiritual and physical fitness started with the scrupulous planning of each day's program and, at the end, its evaluation. My diary, written three weeks after Tony's death, shows a typical record of one day's activity: 6 hours housework and gardening; 4 hours visiting, eating and resting; 2 hours intellectual and spiritual activities; 1 hour helping other people; and 1 hour swimming. Slowly, I began to get on my own feet, thanks to the care of my family and many good friends. Most helpful was a very special Ursuline nun, Sister Marcella Hinz, who lived with me for a couple of years. She encouraged me by her ever-present optimism, and served as an example of kindness, detachment and faith in God.

Perhaps strangely, it was only after a few years that I could look back and appreciate the extraordinary person Tony was. He had an incredible range of interests, evident from all the documentary materials he left behind. Perhaps his greatest loves were poetry and nature. He actively studied many forms of art and crafts, such as painting, music and the making of costume jewellery. These were his frequent gifts to me, family members and friends. His paintings, though not professional, still decorate the walls of my house. Mastering languages, apart from Czech, German and English, was not a problem for him. His Spanish, Italian, Portuguese, Chinese, Japanese textbooks, tapes and dictionaries still fill the bookshelves. In the years before the Internet, he had to have hard copies of reference books in history, geography, literature, mathematics, astrology, biology and botany.

With Tony, there was never a dull moment. When we were still in Prague, both of us hired a private tutor to help us to keep up with the rapid developments in biochemistry and genetics, much to our benefit later in our careers in Canada. Sharing Tony's passions always provided unforgettable experiences. For example, in order to have access to natural reserves out of bounds to the general public in Czechoslovakia, during the Communist era, we decided to join an association of hunters. Both Tony and I had to pass a course required by the association that included a shooting test. The occasion was attended by 100s of men but only by one other woman. Only one gun was available for the test. By the time my turn came, the gun was so hot the problem was not to hit the target but to be able to hold the gun in my hands. Yet without hunters' licenses and occasionally having to share a shabby room at night with men whose odour was difficult to stand, we would not have had the opportunity to discover the beautiful woods nor to encounter the incredible wild animals, whose lives were sacred to us.

Arriving in Toronto at the age of 54 and having to obtain local professional qualifications, Tony did not have enough time to keep up with his research in gastroenterology, an area of medicine in which he was much respected in Czechoslovakia. In Canada, he devoted most of his energy to the practical side of medicine; he was a well-liked physician, especially in the Czech community, where he was a prominent figure in a number of national associations.

Tony's final days were much eased by his reconciliation with his children from his first marriage. His daughter Milena had immigrated to the United States in 1967, from where, around 1990, she moved to Canada with her Jeep and two dogs, Tessie and Uli. Shortly after her arrival, she married Helmut Hitscherich with whom she shared a love of animals, especially dogs and horses. They settled in a lovely house surrounded by woods, evidence perhaps of how much Milena inherited her father's love of nature. Tony's son Jan, who immigrated to the USA after Milena, came to see his father when he was sick. I know this was a source of great comfort to Tony in his last days.

Sister Jarunka in Czechoslovakia in 1998

Jarunka's son, Lukáš Mráz in 1998

23

Returning to the Roots

In 1989, Jiří, my older son, became the first member of our family to visit liberated Czechoslovakia when he travelled there while returning to Canada from Leningrad, where he was designing an amusement park.

Michael, my younger son, was next from the family to return to his country of origin. He published a description of his return in the magazine *Saturday Night* in December 1990, starting with the Velvet Revolution. He wrote:

"In Prague, on November 17,1989, tens of thousands of people – most of them students – marched in memory of Jan Opletal, murdered by the Nazis in 1939. The marchers were met by vicious official force. In the days that followed, the crowds swelled to hundreds of thousands and on November 26, a crowd of half a million people gathered to demand liberty. On November 27, millions went on strike to protest against the government and to support the opposition group Civic Forum. On December 10, the first cabinet in forty-one years without a Communist majority was sworn in."

*Boženka Novotná, author's friend and
neighbour from Podolí, Prague*

*Cousin Jiří Padour, the Bishop of Ceské Budějovice with his
niece Barborka, daughter of cousin Jan Padour*

When my brother Jiří, his wife Milada and daughter Magda travelled to Czechoslovakia from their home in the USA they received a friendly welcome in our native town, Choceň, and especially in the factory our father had founded and owned until it was confiscated by the Communists in 1948. In father's time, the factory probably provided most of the jobs in the region. But since then, productivity had declined owing to incompetent management and unprofitable trade with the USSR. Factory employees took hope in a potential take-over by my brother, who at his birth had been predestined for this post. But, for many reasons, my brother's take-over of the factory in the 1990's did not occur. However, my brother along with Jiří Honig, our school friend, and Josef Koukal, father's former pilot, all veterans of the Second World War, were awarded Honorary Town Citizenship – a distinction delayed for political reasons only by 46 years.

In February 1991 for the first time in 33 years, I returned from Toronto to Prague. I travelled alone as Tony, sadly, was too sick to come along. The plane from Toronto was half empty. At that time, the First Gulf War was raging and people were afraid to travel. The plane came down in Frankfurt, where we had a long wait for the connecting flight to Prague. I was surprised to meet two countrymen, both emigrants to Canada, who were having trouble with the customs in Frankfurt. Neither of them spoke English or German so they were glad for my help interpreting. They came from a younger generation; in my time, we almost always learned German as a second language. Their generation had learned Russian, a language not much used in the West. Their appreciation of my interpreting help was such that they wanted to retain my services as interpreter even in Prague. I was surprised when they could not appreciate that I was totally absorbed anticipating meeting my family and friends after so many years of separation. Once I met the welcoming delegation consisting of my sister, her son Lukáš and our oldest cousin, Váša, there was certainly not even time for me to think about my own emotions on hearing Czech being spoken all around me for the first time in more than two decades.

From the airport, we drove to the centre of Prague. The environment appeared to be not much different from the time Tony and I left the country; everywhere the sorry impacts of Communist rule in the neglect of buildings and streets in our once beautiful capital.

It was not easy to pick up the threads from the past. Too much had happened between the years of 1968 and 1989. Too much pain was associated with the many deaths in the family and among friends. Too much injustice burdened our hearts. On one hand I had not had the full experience of all the wounds inflicted by the regime on my sister as the result of her siblings' illegal escapes, and on account of her family relationship with our cousin Jiří Padour, the priest, who was on the blacklist of priests held by the Communists. I could not fully share with her the fear, suspicion and sheer wrongness, according to all our innate feelings of justice, honesty and love, that she experienced through the years under the Communist dictatorship. On the other hand she could only partly empathise with the difficulties facing not-so-young families, like our brother's and mine, while settling down in completely new environments. The ties with my sister only really started to come together again after glasses of Pilsner beer during an evening in a typical Czech pub!

The impact of communism on the material world was easier to mend than its chilling effects on people's souls. Fear of the secret service and its ubiquitous informers, and the dismissal of religion, played havoc with people's dignity, sincerity, solidarity and compassion. Strangely enough, only in public transport was the behaviour of passengers better than in Western countries. Even the most atrocious looking youngsters would immediately make a seat available for an older person.

Farmers were oppressed during the Communist era more than other sections of the population. A good illustration of this oppression is the case of a prosperous landowner in my grandfather's village. As a member of his social class, he was expelled from the village and forbidden to return, even to attend the funeral of his closest relatives. Taking the risk one night, he secretly visited the grave of his father. He was seen, reported to the authorities and consequently imprisoned.

The story of my uncle Váša Padour, the only sibling of my mother, provides another example of the cruelty and inhumanity of communism. Uncle Váša was the closest relative in my childhood and he shared our home for a while after his parents died. He was smart and funny. The following story has been passed on me by his sons. Uncle Váša loved experimenting and researching. When I was about seven, I was his research subject when he tried to find out the extent of my passion for ice cream. In my home town of Choceň there were three confectioneries and my uncle took me to all three of them, allowing me to choose the kind and amount of ice cream I desired and consumed. Apparently, I did not break a world record and the physiological consequences were as expected.

As the son of a prominent family, uncle Váša was sent to a German language school and to a French Lycée (high school) in Dijon, France. He achieved a Ph.D. in Earth Sciences and taught at the University of Prague. Then Fate played a gruesome trick on him. Shortly after the death of his parents he gave up his academic career because of ill health and in order to fulfill his father's last wish that he move to the family farm. Well-educated, beautiful, gentle Jarmila, from a very good family, became his wife. I remember that when they wanted to share a secret with each other in front of me they would speak French; eagerness to know what they were saying was one of the main reasons why I worked so hard to learn French. They had three sons. I remember the eldest Váša as a two-year-old toddler fearlessly walking between the legs of a big horse in the stables, then climbing a wire fence as naturally as if it was in his nursery.

Such happy days ended when the farm and all the land were confiscated, uncle Váša and his wife Jarmila expelled from their home and a co-operative of the "people" took over. My uncle managed to get a job as a worker in a chemical factory in Pardubice. Each day, he had to walk 5 kms to the train station, ride about half an hour on the train and make a lengthy walk to reach his place of work. Uncle Váša was a very compassionate man but not manually talented. When another worker needed to attend his ailing wife, uncle volunteered to take over his duty. Tragically, he was caught in the explosion of a nitric acid basin and was burned from his neck down. He survived this horrific accident, but his active life was over.

Váša, my uncle's eldest son, was denied access to education beyond the basic nine years of schooling because he was a son of a farmer. He was constantly being told by the Communists that he was the enemy of the people and this sadistic accusation marked him his whole life. First, he joined his father in the chemical factory then, after his father's accident he left the factory and he took on any job, such as a driver, that would allow him to look after his parents. Despite very good looks and a kind nature, he remained single all his life.

All three of uncle Váša's boys found a haven with their two aunts who lived in Prague in their own villas. In a sense the aunts welcomed the opportunity of having additional persons in each of their houses because, under the Communist regime, the allowance of living space was only 12 square metres per person and they might otherwise have been forced out of their homes.

Fortunately, the "curse" of the boys' origin did not travel fast enough to prevent the younger two sons from continuing their studies. Jan, the middle one, studied engineering and escaped to the United States before finishing his studies. There he worked in landscaping, married and had three children, Matthew, Peter and Barbara. He was the only one of the three cousins with whom I could be in contact while in Canada.

The story of the youngest cousin, Jiří, is the most exciting one for me because he followed the life of the spirit. Cousin Jiří was only six years older than my own son, another Jiří. Brought up with two tough brothers, he felt sympathy for his young cousin, who at that time was an only child. He took my son camping, which seems to be one of bright episodes in the memory of the youngster. Cousin Jiří was apprenticed with the Holerith Company as a manual worker but then managed to get into drama school, and as an actor he worked in the theatre "Na Zábradlí" along with Václav Havel. Neither of them dreamed that one day they would be living next to each other under the most unusual circumstances. Havel, by then a famous playwright, became president of the Czech Republic living in Prague Castle. Jiří, at that time an assistant bishop, could see his friend from his window in the neighbouring palace of the archbishop.

While still performing in the theatre, Jiří received a scholarship to study at the Sorbonne in Paris. There he underwent a change of heart. On his return to Prague he entered a seminary, and after completing his studies joined the Capuchin Friars. At that time, still under the Communist regime, the church was out of favour with the Party and churches were in great disrepair. Jiří, ever the athlete, repaired more than one crumbling church building, including their roofs. After the liberation, Jiří was put in charge of one of the most precious buildings in Prague, known as the "Loreta", a famous historical shrine of Our Lady of Loreto. Under the Communists the building had been the seat of the secret service and was in a pitiful state of repair. For example, the beautiful ceilings were covered by wiring. In the beginning Jiří was a one-man show and had to be the doorman, repair man, administrator and priest. I saw the place in its run-down state and later when restored to its full glory, all thanks to the labour and perseverance of Jiří.

I remember an embarrassing incident when Jiří was appointed an assistant bishop in Prague. We went for a walk and it started to rain. All of a sudden Jiří pulled out a piece of paper from his pocket and asked me, "Would you like to see 'Nabucco'? It's playing tonight in the Cathedral of Saint Vít and I'm supposed to make the introduction. These are my notes," he said. I was speechless. This was an opportunity I could not have dreamed of; my favourite composer Verdi, in his most dramatic opera with the religious theme of the exile of Jews to Babylon, performed in the dim light and awesome atmosphere of the most famous Czech Cathedral. Of course I wanted to go.

We went directly from the park to the Cathedral. I was still in my raincoat, all wet, including my hair. We were let in through a side door and I was seated in the front row among the top government officials and their wives. I did not mind that, being absorbed in the brilliant performance of the opera. My embarrassment came later. After the show my cousin casually said, "Let's join the crowd in the bar of Vikárka." A waiter at the door of the restaurant offered us champagne. Ahead of us were the minister's wives in their long, elegant robes. I was introduced to them and while shaking hands felt the ladies gazing with astonishment at my wet raincoat, wet shoes and wet hair. I was glad when we disappeared fast.

Cousin Jiří was next appointed Bishop of České Budějovice, a region neighbouring Austria. I met him when he came as the head of the Czech delegation to the Catholic World Youth Meeting in Toronto in 2002. He took some time to meet, for the first time, my son Jiří's family; Simone, his wife, and their children, 15-year-old Jean-Marc, 12-year-old Tom and 5-year-old Majka. The two men, an uncle and a nephew, both called Jiří were named after their godfather, my brother Jiří. They enjoyed talking about the time when as boys they went camping together.

My first return visit to Czechoslovakia in 1991 was only for one week so I did not have enough time to learn about all of my close relatives. I did enquire about my aunt Anežka, father's only sister, who lived to the blessed age of 90. The last years of her life were under stressful cirumstances. She sold her house with the condition of keeping a room for herself and receiving help when needed. However, the latter was not given. She spent her last days in a dirty, smelly room in an old people's home, where she was moved by a Communist social worker, on account of her capitalist origin. The only person from among the relatives and friends who lived in Choceň at that time and who came regularly to visit and look after aunt Anežka was my deceased uncle Josef's housekeeper, Růženka. She was a tiny lady, with a golden heart and also an excellent cook. She served

212   FAITH AND HOPE

my uncle, a long-time divorcee, while he lived in his tastefully designed house, situated next to his factory. She did not abandon him when the Communists confiscated all his property and sent him to the uranium mines. She continued to look after him until his death from lung cancer. In her care, kind Růženka went far beyond the call of a servant's duty.

My sister Jarunka, an architect, once described by my younger son Michael as an "elegant blonde", was always moving at a terrific speed, even when visiting art exhibitions, going to concerts, operas, or skiing in Switzerland, Austrian or the Italian Alps. She also exercised conscientiously in the gym twice a week, as well as attending daily mass at the Cathedral of St. Marketa.

Jarunka's ascent as an architect was anything but easy. After concluding high school studies in Fine Arts and Graphics, she was accepted at the highly selective Academy of Fine Arts and Architecture, thanks to her outstanding scholastic performance. Eventually she was able to win a substantial scholarship. After graduation, she continued working with professor Benš and architect Podzemný on the reconstruction of the Prague Castle gardens and within a year she won a competition to be an architect at the National Art Gallery, located in Prague Castle. In this position, she became a colleague of Anna Masaryk, daughter of the first president of Czechoslovakia, Tomáš Garigue Masaryk. The National Gallery collection included works by such famous artists as J. Zrzavý, J. Stursa, J. Preisler, J. Navrátil, Hollar, Rodin, Michelangelo Buonarotti, Henry Moore, Friedrich Schiller and Max Švabinský. Within seven years, she organized at least 60 exhibitions and permanent art instalments at the National Gallery. Jarunka became well-known for installations in the main Czech galleries of works of Baroque and Gothic, Medieval, Modern Art, as well as the Cubistic Work of Otto Gutfreund. Other exhibitions included Japanese woodcarvings, African, American and Asian Ceramics, and a History of Prague. Jarunka also cooperated on a number of other projects, such as the illumination of the Czech castle Karlstejn, as well as in several architectonic competitions. As a successful artist she had the rare privilege of travelling on business outside the country up to the Soviet invasion. While in Belgium she met Mr. Franz Westerveld who became her good friend and the father of her only child Lukáš. Jarunka was an exemplary mother, as demonstrated by Lukáš's later achievements.

Jarunka changed the direction of her career as an architect by joining the Office of the Chief Architect of Prague and began working to protect the city's historical buildings and approve new ones so that they would fit in the existing environment. She found this work rewarding. No wonder she now knows Prague like the palm of her hand.

The experience in city planning proved to be especially valuable after 1989 when the new democratic government agreed to pay restitution to the original owners of properties confiscated by the Communist regime. Jarunka fought bravely with the help of three lawyers to retrieve at least some parts of father's property. She had to quit her job to engage in the battle with the suffocating red tape, the weapon of the inefficient civil servants. She was even complimented by one of them, who told her, "Miss Mrázová, you are unique. Many applicants like you gave up their rights, totally exasperated with the snags of legalities, but not you!"

The compensation that was eventually paid has allowed Jarunka to acquire two smart condominiums in a good area of

Prague for herself and for her son Lukáš. She managed to recover our farm (which was totally destroyed) and gave it to her son who is rebuilding it for his family. After repossessing uncle's Josef's factory, she passed it on to my son Jiří and to my brother's son Jára. The financial compensation she divided conscientiously among the three siblings, my brother, herself and myself. Thanks to her hard work and persistence, she makes me feel prosperous when I open my Czech bank account. Her efforts to regain our parents' heritage took more then 15 years and a toll on her health.

Jarunka's loyalty to her family has included not only caring for our dying father and mother but also for their burials. She even volunteered to take care of my husband's parents' remains, at the time when the cemetery where they were buried was discontinued and Tony, as a political refugee, was barred from entering Czechoslovakia. It was an act of mercy by Jarunka to transfer the remains from Brno to our family grave in Choceň.

After 1989, my old friend Jaryna Jeništová, the daughter of father's factory manager, was very helpful in our fight to recover title to our family's possessions. She began working in the family business in 1942 and since that time had been working in the factory and knew all the employees. After the fall of Communism, many of them seemed anxious to get on my family's good side, but all of them brought only disappointment. Jaryna was my family's best ally. Sadly, she died in 1999.

Before my sister acquired her condominium in 1996, I stayed with Milena Drtinová in Letná when visiting Prague. She was one of the young people my father employed during the war to save from forced labour in Germany. Her husband Mirek, a physician, in turn saved my father from prison. While I was married to Karel we were good friends.

Milena came to visit us in Canada and my brother in the States after the death of her husband in the 1980s. One night, while with me at the cottage, we had a visit from a family of raccoons. Raccoons do not occur in Europe and Milena never forgot this incident, especially after father raccoon knocked on the door and we saw his eyes glowing in the dark.

After Milena downsized her apartment in 1997, I used to stay in Prague with Boženka, my former neighbour in Podolí. We reminisced for hours, recalling her help with my domestic tasks, especially her care for Michael. She believed I gave her courage to manage her demanding family. Boženka came to visit me in Toronto. Once, while staying at the cottage, we had help there from a young Mexican called José. To ease Boženka's climb up a hill where we used to sit in the evenings, José wanted to build steps to please her. For that purpose he used large rocks which supported a telephone pole; I was horrified and expected the pole to collapse; fortunately it did not and the pole is still standing ten years later.

When in Prague I always visit Karel's grave. It is an occasion to spend time with his nieces Zdena and Libuše; they call me "auntie" although we are the same age. It is a joke between us, dating back to our first encounter in 1946; it breaks down the barrier built up by the long pauses between our meetings. There are visits to family graves in Choceň; the graves are always in perfect condition, thanks to Jaroslava, contemporary of my son Jiří and the daughter of Josef Dvořáček, our gardener from before the Second World War. Jaroslava's daughter Hedvika visited us in Canada and took English lessons, one year before she got married. She now has two sons. I love to visit the whole family. In their environment, the spirit of my parents seems closer than anywhere else.

Author's children and grandchildren:
Jiří with wife Simone (right) and children Jean-Marc,
Tom and Majka; and Michael with wife Lucia and
daughter Milena (front left)

24

New Shoots on the Family Tree

M y two sons, Jiří and Michael, did not experience so-called normal family lives, such as my siblings and I did. Normal life does not necessarily mean an uneventful life, rather a life embraced and supported by extended family.

Jiří was essentially an orphan looked after by his grandmother while I was working. He has his father Karel's drive and his grandfather's desire for adventure. Jiří adored his grandfather Mráz who, for the short time he lived, was a substitute for his deceased father. The influence of Jiří's kind, disciplined, Christian grandmother gave him a firm foothold lasting him into his maturity as a husband and father. God must have given special protection to Jiří; how could he otherwise have survived two major car accidents, the first as an infant when his father was tragically killed, and later as a teenager, being run over by a truck?

Jiří was fortunate to have the help of his aunt Jarunka to start his carrier in the study of architecture in Prague, and the help of our friend Marjorie Hayman in England to complete his studies in London. His interest in environmental issues, which began in England, has now become his successful enterprise in healthy housing in North America. Always enthusiastic for new experiences, he fulfilled his teenage desire to see the world by applying his professional skills in the Middle East, crossing the Atlantic in a small sailboat, and by attending professional conferences all over the world. Jiří was lucky to find the right partner, Simone, and together they have succeeded in achieving a happy family with sons Jean-Marc and Tom, and daughter Majka.

Michael also had a disjoined childhood. He seemed to inherit his talents for art from his grandmother Margareta, a concert pianist, on his father's side. Unfortunately, she died before Michael was born. From his father, Michael acquired the need for independence and self-sufficiency. This created challenges for him when, at the age of eight, our family arrived in Canada and he had to make new friends and integrate himself into a new culture. His achievements at the University of Toronto School decided his career. His teacher encouraged him to become an artist. On reading his essays and plays, I assumed that he would succeed better as a writer. With either choice, I worried how he would earn his living. His reaction to my concerns was to qualify as a chef and this expertise supported him through his years in New York City at Cooper's Union, the art school. He shared his love of New York City with his half-sister Milena. He uses his many talents not only in cuisine, but in visual art, writing and teaching. With his second wife Lucia, he shares the support of the family and the care of their daughter Milena.

I have been blessed more than the majority of grandmothers. Not only do I admire my very capable daughters-in-law, Simone and Lucia, but their mothers are my closest friends.

Simone's mother Dorothy has been my friend since our years in university together in England. Lucia's mother, Lucia Senior, is a colleague, a university teacher, with whom I share the trials and joys of our professional experiences.

There is only one of God's gifts greater than children and this is the gift of grandchildren. With them one may learn what genuine love is.

Author in recent years

25

The Spiritual Journey

An appropriate reading in the Lenten season is Psalm 19, "The law of the Lord is perfect, reviving the soul; His commandments are the wisdom of the simple." I could not have understood these words at an earlier age. At home, we did not read the Bible. At school we learned the Catechism. Mother's bedtime reading was "The Imitation of Christ" by Thomas á Kempis and in time all three of her children were given copies of this book. My mother walked in the steps of her mother, a true Catholic.

I did not differentiate religion and spirituality until late in my adulthood. The Roman Catholic Church had a strong impact on my early childhood, on life at school and on the whole of my culture. It influenced the daily, weekly and yearly ways of conduct, activities, even the style of dressing. There were prayer times, morning and night, Sunday church and Marian celebrations in the evenings of May. Regardless of the weather, on Easter Sunday we would discard the hated long stockings held up by uncomfortable garters and only put them on again on All Saints Day, on November 1st. The ceremony of Confirmation was much celebrated. Fasting at the appropriate times and seasons was strictly respected, as were seasonal confessions and Holy Communion. Religion was not something one thought about, one just went along with its program.

The beginning of the change in my approach to spirituality began when I left home at the age of 15 and arrived in England. I found it confusing that people lived so differently to the way I was brought up. It started to be difficult to follow the usual routine, not in private prayers but in participating in the life of the Church. The first school I went to was Anglican, not so different in spirit from the one I was used to, only the emphasis was on Scripture more than the Eucharist. Next was the boarding school run by the Quakers, who were godly and good people. We had morning Bible reading and sacred music. The food was vegetarian and the spirit of the school was totally ecumenical. At that time, I attended Mass very rarely but continued to pray. I prayed very intensely on the occasions of mortal danger, and during the war when my brother, in the RAF, was flying over France.

All religions were banned under the Communist regime; spiritual life was a very private affair. In Canada, I was first drawn into the Anglican Church before eventually returning to the Roman Catholic Church, the church of my forefathers. It was at this point that I began to distinguish between religiosity and spirituality, between Catholicism and catholicity.

The events leading to my inner transformation were influenced by my friend Dorothy, already mentioned a few times in these memoirs. In the early 1980s, Dorothy chose the life of a hermit and lived in the woods near Moncton, New Brunswick.

On one occasion she came to a charismatic conference in Toronto and took me along. I could not relate well to the spirit of the occasion, but a few days later, on August 16, 1976, at 8.45 am, I had a peculiar experience. I was sitting in the garden of Victoria College on the University of Toronto campus. From nowhere, I saw a flash of light sharply dividing the space into black and white. That moment, I interpreted what I was seeing as the separation of white Truth from black Lie. I took it as an enlightenment liberating me from the dim, grey world of half-truths which had prevailed everywhere under the Communist regime.

After this incident, my inner life began to change. One of the inspirations came from a book Dorothy lent me, entitled "The Way of a Pilgrim". Dorothy also directed me to an Ursuline nun, Sister Marcella Hinz, who helped in my spiritual growth and in other ways. It was Marcella who arranged a Catholic Church wedding for Tony and I. Many times we met with Marcella in the Church of St. Basil where we prayed together over our past misfortunes. Slowly, I started to see life and myself in a new light. It was with Marcella's help that I survived the sad, long years of my husband Tony's terminal illness.

Tony and I were also given a great spiritual uplift by a male nurse, Brian Muskow, when he was looking after Tony during the final stage of his illness. Brian saw our desperation and tried to help by introducing us to Eastern ways of meditation. This was the first time I learned about listening to God, instead of only talking. He told me about a Californian group, Blue Mountain Meditation Center, founded by Sri Eknath Easwaran, a Professor of English of East Indian origin, who taught a meditation course at Berkeley University. The meditation course was practical and consisted of an eight-point program:

meditating, transfer energy from the meditation, slowing down, one-pointed attention, training the senses, putting others first, seeking spiritual companionship and reading the mystics.

The practical program of Professor Easwaran helped me to improve the quality of my time with God, and to understand better the teachings of my religion. It continues to help me on the last stretch of my pilgrimage on this earth.

If I am expected to conclude this account of my life with "pearls of wisdom", what I can say, in the briefest summary, is that a person's life is always worthwhile, especially when it leads to the discovery of the ever-present Spirit expanding our consciousness. Awareness of God may come in many forms, and have many expressions; what endures through them all is our faith and hope in the supremacy of good over evil. This book is my testament to that.

Appendix

Published Work in Refereed Journals

Taylor, J.P., Krondl, M., Csima, A. Symptom relief and adherence in the rotary diversified diet, a treatment for environmental illness. Alternative Therapies in Health and Medicine. 10(4):58-65, 2004.

Krondl, M., Lau, D., Coleman, C., Stocker, G. Tayloring of nutritional support for older adults in the community. Journal of Nutrition for the Elderly. 23(2):17-32, 2003.

Taylor, J.P., Krondl, M., Spidel, M., Csima, A. Dietary adequacy of the rotary diversified diet as a treatment for environmental illness. Canadian Journal of Dietetic Practice and Research. 63:198-201, 2002.

Krondl, M., Coleman, P., Bradley, C.L., Lau, D., Ryan, N. Subjectively healthy elderly consuming a nutrition supplement maintained body mass index and improved some nutritional parameters and perceived well-being. Journal of the American Dietetic Association. 99:1542-1548, 1999.

Taylor, J.P., Krondl, M., Csima, A. Assessing adherence to a rotary diversified diet, a treatment for environmental illness. Journal of the American Dietetic Association. 98:1439-1444, 1998.

Taylor, J.P. and Krondl, M. Environmental illness. Canadian Home Economics Journal. 47:160-165, 1997.

Fogler-Levitt, E., Lau, D., Csima, A., Krondl, M., Coleman, P. Utilization of home delivered meals by recipients 75+ years of age or older. Journal of the American Dietetic Association. 95: 552-557, 1995.

Lau, D., Coleman, P., Krondl, M. Meals on Wheels in Ontario, Canada: Development of Nutritional Standards. Age & Nutrition. 5:22-27, 1994.

Rusen, J., Krondl, M., Csima, A. Perceived chewing satisfaction and food use of older adults. Journal of the Canadian Dietetic Association. 54:88-91, 1993.

Parent, M.E. and Krondl, M. Reconstruction of past calcium intake patterns during adulthood. Journal of the American Dietetic Association. 93:649-652, 1993.

Parker, S.L. and Krondl, M. Foods perceived as causing adverse reactions among adults. Journal of the American Dietetic Association. 93:40-44, 1993.

Owen, R., Krondl, M., Csima, A. Impact of emotional depression on nutrient intake of elderly recipients of home delivered meals. Journal of the Canadian Dietetic Association. 53:24-29, 1992.

Parker, S.L., Garner, D.M., Krondl, M. Psychological characteristics of patients with reported adverse reactions to foods. International Journal of Eating Disorders. 10:433-439, 1991.

Parker, S.L., Sussman, G.L., Tarlo, S., Leznoff, A., Krondl, M. Characteristics of patients with food related complaints. The Journal of Allergy and Clinical Immunology. 86:503-511, 1990.

Jerzsa-Latta, M., Krondl, M., Coleman, P. Use and perceived attributes of Cruciferous vegetables in terms of genetically-mediated taste sensitivity. Appetite. 15:127-134, 1990.

Krondl, M. Living with sensory loss: Smell and taste. Writings in Gerontology. The National Advisory Council on Aging. March, 1990. Pp.21-38.

Taylor, J., Krondl, M., Rao, V. Acetylsalicylic acid dose fails to affect energy intake of osteoarthritic elderly. Journal of Nutrition for the Elderly. 8:79-96, 1989.

Parker, S.L., Sussman, G.L., Krondl, M. Dietary aspects of adverse reactions to food in adults. Canadian Medical Association Journal. 139:711-718, 1988.

Niewind, A.C., Krondl, M., Lau, D. Relative impact of selected factors on food choices of elderly individuals. Canadian Journal of Aging. 7:32-46, 1988.

Niewind, A., Krondl, M., Shrott, M. Genetic influences on the selection of Brassica vegetables by elderly individuals. Nutrition Research. 8:13-20, 1988.

Krondl, M. and Coleman, P. Aging in Canada: A nutritional perspective. Canadian Home Economics Journal. 37:119-124, 1987.

Kennedy, J. and Krondl, M. Evaluation of the dietary adequacy of elderly osteoarthritic individuals treated with acetylsalicylic acid. Journal of the Canadian Dietetic Association. 48:232-237, 1987.

Niewind, A.C., Krondl, M., Van't Foort, T. Combinations of foods in terms of their compatibility. Ecology of Food and Nutrition. 19:131-139, 1986.

Zimmerman, S. and Krondl, M. Perceived intolerance of vegetables among the elderly. Journal of the American Dietetic Association. 86:1047-1051, 1986.

Hrboticky, N. and Krondl, M. Dietary acculturation process of Chinese adolescent immigrants. Nutrition Research. 5:1185, 1985.

Krondl, M. and Coleman, P. Towards greater nutritional adequacy in advancing years. Geriatric Medicine. 1:44, 1985.

Hrboticky, N. and Krondl, M. Acculturation to Canadian foods of Chinese immigrant boys: change in perceived flavour, health value and prestige of foods. Appetite. 5:117-126, 1984.

Krondl, M., Coleman, P., Wade, J., Milner, J. A twin study examining the genetic influence on food-related behaviour. Human Nutrition: Applied Nutrition. 37A:189-198, 1983.

Lynde, B., Krondl, M., Lau, D., Coleman, P. Food habits of Italians in Toronto. Nutrition Research. 3:265-270, 1983.

George, R. and Krondl, M. The perceptions and the food use of adolescent boys and girls. Nutrition and Behavior. 1:115, 1983.

Yurkiw, M.A., Krondl, A., Krondl, M. Anthropometric and dietary assessment of select single living urban elderly. Journal of Nutrition for the Elderly. 2:3-15, 1983.

Wong, H., Krondl, M., Williams, J.I. Long term effect of a nutrition intervention program for the elderly. Journal of Nutrition for the Elderly. 2:32-48, 1982.

Krondl,M., Lau,D., Yurkiw, M., Coleman, P.H. Food use and perceived food meanings of the elderly. Journal of the American Dietetic Association. 80:523-529, 1982.

Krondl, M., George, R., Coleman, P. Factors influencing food selection of adolescents in different social environments. Nutrition Quarterly. 6:38-43, 1982.

Krondl, M., Coleman, P. Geriatric nutrition. Prevention Review. 3:2-4, 1981.

Coleman, P. and Krondl, M. Recruitment of free-living elderly for nutrition research. Journal of the Canadian Dietetic Association. 42:352-358, 1981.

Wade, J., Milner, J., Krondl, M. Evidence for a physiological regulation of food selection and nutrient intake in twins. American Journal of Clinical Nutrition. 3(1):1-7, 1979.

Krondl, M. and Floyd, B. Social and psychological aspects of selection and consumption of some dairy products by the elderly. Nutrition Quarterly. 3(1):1-7, 1979.

Lau, D., Hanada, L., Kaminsky, O., Krondl, M. Predicting food use by measuring attitudes and preference. Food Product Development. May, 1979. Pp.66-72.

Reaburn, J., Krondl, M., Lau, D. Social determinants in food selection. Journal of the American Dietetic Association. 74:637-641, 1979.

Smicklas-Wright, H. and Krondl, M. Dietary counselling and the behavioural sciences. Journal of the Canadian Dietetic Association. 40(2):99-103, 1979.

Krondl, M. and Lau, D. Food habit modifications as a public health measure. Canadian Journal of Public Health. 69(1):39-43, 1978.

Read, D., Gottschalk, P., Albergaria, A., Krondl, M., Berkoff, F., Cabsck, N., McDonald, M. Journal Survey Results. Journal of the Canadian Dietetic Association. 38(3):180-182, 1977.

Wong, R., Holowaty, M., Krondl, M., Lau, D. The effect of culturally determined satiety meaning on food practices. Journal of the Canadian Dietetic Association. 37(4) 245, 1976.

Boxen, G. and Krondl, M. Anthropometry as a tool in motivating weight reduction. Journal of the Canadian Dietetic Association. 34:204-209, 1973.

Savage, W.E.and Krondl, M. A nutritional investigation of Canadian parasitized in the tropics. Journal of the Canadian Dietetic Association. 33:55-63, 1972.

Krondl, M. The Cause and Effect of Starvation and Malnutrition. Audio-Visual Teaching Aid. Instructional Media Services, University of Toronto, 1975. (Reviewed by Konishi, F. Journal of Nutrition Education 8:37, 1976).

Krondl, M., Hrubý, J. Nutritive values of potatoes in Czechoslovakia. Československá Hygiena. 13:159-163, 1968.

Hrubý, J., Sedláček, B., Krondl, M. The assessment of the nutritive values of food by the regional medical laboratories. Čs Gastroenterologie. 21:475-481, 1967.

Hrubý, J., Krondl, M., Sedláček, B. Nutritive values of milk. Výživa Lidu. 22:80, 1967.

Šmrha, O., Škopková, M. The impact of food consumption patterns on the development of food industry. Průmysl Potravin. 8:232-234, 1957.

Škopková, M. The role of nutrition research in meat processing. Průmysl Potravin. 7:444-449, 1956.

Čapková, M., Škopková, M. Nutritive values of flour produced in Czechoslovakia. Průmysl Potravin. 6:501-503, 1955.

Škopková, M., Bažant, V., Miksa, J. Dental caries and nutritional status of rural and urban children. Časopis Lékařů Ceských. 9:39, 1954.

Škopková, M. Regional differences in the nutritive values of tomatoes. Výživa Lidu; 9:103, 1954.

Hrubá, M., Škopková, M., Šmrha, O. Food consumption of workers in hot environments. Sborník pro pathofyziologii trávení a výživy. 9:62, 1953.

Škopková, M., Šmrha, O. Food consumption of athletes in selected categories. Výživa Lidu. 7:105, 1952.

Škopková, M. Physiology of nutrition in food industry. Průmysl Potravin. 3:301-304, 1952.

Chapters, Symposia and Proceedings

Krondl, M. and Lau, D. Acculturation of Food Habits. In: Health and Cultures. Masi, R., Mensah, L.L., McLead, K. (Eds.) Mosaic Press Publication. Vol. 1, 1. 1993.

Krondl, M. Living with Sensory Loss: Smell and Taste. Writings in Gerontology. The National Advisory Council on Aging. 1990.

Krondl, M. Conceptual Models. In: Anderson, G.H. Diet and Behaviour. London: Springer-Verlag, 1990. Pp. 5-16.

Krondl, M. Food habits determinants of North American
adolescents: nutritional implications. In: L'Alimentation des
Adolescents. Health Department of Interprofessional Centre for
Dairy Documentation and Information. Paris, France. 1988.
Pp. 111-117.

Krondl, M. and Coleman, P. The role of food perceptions in food
use. In: Control of Appetite, Winick, M. (ed.). Current Concepts in
Nutrition. Vol. 16, 1988. Pp. 53-78.

Parker, S. and Krondl, M. Dietary implications of adverse food
reactions to foods in adults. In: Food Allergy. Chandra, R.K (ed.)
Nutrition Research, Education Foundation. St. John's,
Newfoundland. 1987. Pp. 287-304.

Krondl, M. and Coleman, P. Social and biocultural determinants
of food selection. In: Progress in Food and Nutrition Science. R.K.
Chandra (ed.) Pergamon Press. 1986. Pp. 179-203

Krondl, M. and Coleman, P. Food selection and dietary intake of
elderly persons. In: Nutrition, Immunity and Illness. Chandra,
R.K. (ed.). Pergamon Press. 1985. Pp. 34-42.

Krondl, M. and Hrboticky, N. Adapting to cultural change to
food habits. In: Malnutrition: Determinants and Consequences.
Proceedings of Western Hemisphere Nutrition Congress VII.
Alan R. Liss, Inc. 1984. Pp.221-229.

Krondl, M., George, R., Coleman, P. Food perceptions in the dietary
behaviour of the adolescent. In: Proceedings of the International
Symposium on Adolescent Nutrition and Food Behaviour of June,
1982. University of Prince Edward Island. 1984. Pp. 115-130.

Lau, D., Krondl, M. Coleman, P. Psychological factors affecting food
selection. In: Nutrition and Behaviour. Galler, J. R (ed.) Plenum
Publishing Corporation. 1984. Pp. 397-416.

Krondl, M. and Lau, D. Social determinants in human food selection.
In: The Psychobiology of Human Food Selection. Barker, L.M. (ed.)
AVI, 1982. Pp. 139-152.

Krondl, M. A new method in food selection of the elderly in Western society. In: Nutrition and Food Science. Santos, W., Lopes, N., Barbosa, J.J., Chaves, D., Valente, J.C.(Eds.) Plenum Publishing Corporation. 1980. Vol. 33. Pp. 777-785.

Krondl, M. and Boxen, G.G. Nutrition behaviour, food resources and energy. In: Gastronomy. The Anthropology of Food and Food Habits. Arnott, M.L. The Hague. Mouton Publishers. 1975. Pp. 113-120.

Krondl, M. and Welsh, J. Toward a dynamic aspects of nutrition behaviour. In: Proceedings of the 9th International Congress of Nutrition, Mexico. Karger, Basel. 1975. Vol. 4. Pp. 283-289.

Books

Krondlová, M., Lhotská, E. Physical and Chemical Changes in Foods on Processing. Pedagogical Publishers. Prague, 1967.

Krondlová – Škopková, M., Šmrha, O. Food Composition Tables. Third revised edition. National Health Publishers. Prague, 1965.

Škopková, M., Šmrha, O., Váša, J. Food Composition Tables. Second revised edition. National Health Publishers. Prague, 1957.

Škopková, M. Food Composition Tables. First edition. Food Industry Publishers. Prague, 1952.